A Cock and Bull for Kitty

Published by Telford Publications*

Design by 875 *Design*
Illustrations by David Eccles

© George Morrow 2011
Telford Publications
301 Mill Stream Way,
Williamsburg, VA, U.S.A., 23185

Tel (757) 565-7215
Fax (757) 565-7216
e-mail contact@telfordpublications.com
www.telfordpublications.com

FIRST EDITION

*Telford Publications is named for Alexander Telford,
a volunteer rifleman from Rockbridge County, Virginia, who
served in three Revolutionary War campaigns, in the last of which,
Yorktown, he was personally recognized by Gen. George Washington
for his extraordinary marksmanship with the long rifle.

ISBN 978-0-9831468-0-3
Printed and bound by Sheridan Press, 450 Fame Avenue, Hanover, PA

A Cock and Bull
for Kitty

Lord Dunmore and the Affair
that Ruined the
British Cause in Virginia

George Morrow

WILLIAMSBURG IN CHARACTER

John Murray, Lord Dunmore, age 35
*"In his Guards uniform, best foot forward
to show his well-turned calf"*

For Joan

"If a man could say nothing against a character but what he can prove, history could not be written."
SAMUEL JOHNSON

Contents

Preface

Poor Lord Dunmore, frustrated by British ministers who failed to grasp the seriousness of the threat to his authority and despised by American patriots who viewed him as little more than a perfidious Scot, Dunmore is remembered today chiefly as the last royal governor of Virginia whose inept government helped push the colony into open rebellion. Was he simply unlucky to be appointed when relations between America and Great Britain were rapidly deteriorating? Or was he the author of his own misfortunes by his consistent failure to exercise discretion in both his personal and public life at a time when the fate of the British Empire in America hung in the balance?

John Murray, fourth earl of Dunmore, was an experienced military officer and career administrator. He had become a faithful servant of the crown following a royal pardon for his support of Prince Charles Edward Stuart ("Bonnie Prince Charlie") during the '45. He joined his uncle John's regiment, the Third Foot Guards in 1749 and served in campaigns against the French during the Seven Years War before returning to his estates in Scotland following his marriage to Charlotte Stewart, daughter of the earl of Galloway in 1759. Two years later, he was elected one of the Scottish peers in the House of Lords, which brought him into the heart of London's social and political life shortly after George III ascended the throne. Over the next few years, Dunmore became dissatisfied with prospects at home and began considering putting himself forward for an office in America. Allied to the duke of

Bedford's faction in Parliament through his wife's family, he eventually achieved his wishes in 1770 when appointed governor of New York.

Dunmore found New York much to his liking and quickly set about amassing a large estate in the western part of the colony on Lake Champlain. There was nothing unusual in government officers feathering their own nests while conducting public affairs and Dunmore differed from others only in his undisguised eagerness to reap as much benefit from his position as quickly as possible. Nor was there anything unusual in his taking a mistress, the young and attractive Kitty Eustace, especially given that he had been separated from his wife and young family, who remained in Scotland awaiting his word to join him. Such practices were tolerated providing they did not interfere with the efficient administration of the crown's business and as long as the officers carried themselves with dignity and honor. Judged by this standard, Dunmore failed spectacularly.

In this sparkling and wonderfully-crafted essay, George Morrow turns the spotlight on one important example of Dunmore's tortuous relationship with Virginia: his involvement in the court proceedings of *Blair* v. *Blair*. Much to Dunmore's annoyance, not long after settling into his position in New York he had been appointed to the governorship of Virginia to replace the highly popular Lord Botetourt, but dragged his feet and did not arrive in Williamsburg until September 1771. Under Morrow's close reading, the new governor is revealed as a man of simple affections, loyal to his friends, who enjoyed good company and wine. For all the trappings of royal office he remained at heart a bluff, military man, most at ease with other military men, such as George Washington, with whom he often went riding, dined, and went to the theater. He disliked duplicity, although not above it himself, and detested those who he believed had abused his trust. Quick of temper, he was frequently incapable of restraining his passions, which gave the impression of an arrogant and overbearing temperament. There was little subtlety about Lord Dunmore in his political dealings.

And yet, had the times been different he might well have won at least the grudging approval of Virginians. He was not an inflexible bureaucrat toeing the British line, and in his anxiety to acquire western lands he had much in common with many of the colony's elite. On a couple of occasions, British ministers had to caution Dunmore about aligning himself too closely with Virginia rather than royal interests. His own involvement in waging war against the Shawnee in 1774 and the determination to uphold Virginia's claims to western territories against those of Pennsylvania gained the widespread support of frontier communities and the Virginia gentry who had long hoped to exploit the spacious territories of the Ohio Valley. Caught up in the gathering imperial crisis on the eve of the Revolution, however, Dunmore amply demonstrated that did not possess the political dexterity or skill to negotiate the various political forces in play.

Kitty Eustace Blair, the governor's mistress, offers a perfect counterpoint, and Morrow does a wonderful job in uncovering this remarkable woman, who is virtually unknown to us. She was not the wife of a famous patriot and left no corpus of literature or letters, only faint echoes of her vivacious character and finely-tuned mind. In her marriage to the young Dr. James Blair and the subsequent scandal that blighted her first few years in Williamsburg, it is all too easy to dismiss her as a scheming gold digger, intent on securing a valuable annuity from her hapless husband. But what comes through forcefully, in Morrow's treatment, is her strong sense of rectitude and adroitness in handling the challenges she (and other women) faced in the male-dominated society of the eighteenth century. She was an expert in sexual politics, using her charm, intelligence, and wit to over-come her severest critics. Everyone liked Kitty.

The central plot of the essay revolves around the court case of *Blair* v. *Blair* that captivated Williamsburg and Virginia society between 1771 and 1773. Morrow romps through the salacious details of the case to bring us back to the world of Kitty, her feisty widowed mother, Margaret, the unfortunate James Blair and, of course, Lord Dunmore. To this cast of characters, Morrow adds the finest array of legal talent the colony had to offer: the conservative Attorney General, John Randolph, and firebrand Patrick Henry appearing on behalf of Kitty Eustace Blair and her mother, and on the other side, James Mercer, Thomas Jefferson, and Edmund Pendleton representing the aristocratic Blairs. It was, as Morrow asserts, a newspaperman's dream, involving a wealthy and long-established family of impeccable reputation, a distressed, young and attractive wife, and the most intimate sexual details pertaining to the ill-fated newlyweds. The upshot turns out to be as unpredictable as the causes of the action in the first place.

The case itself and what it reveals about Williamsburg high society in the early 1770s would be worthy of a study in their own right, but Morrow is more ambitious and focuses instead on what the scandal tells us about two quite different views of authority before the outbreak of the Revolution, epitomized in the moral sensibilities of the two protagonists, Kitty Eustace Blair and Dunmore. The recognition of authority without moral basis or rationale was to Kitty's mind mere unquestion-ing subservience. Virginia's patriots, no more than Kitty, would not accept authority, whether in Williamsburg or London, which was believed unjust. The grounds for acceptance of royal authority were shifting: a development that Dunmore never came close to understanding. The author's sensitive and persuasive argument on this theme is a *tour de force*.

Dunmore's career never fully recovered from his failure in Virginia. He returned to Scotland in 1776 and continued to hope that the British would eventually recapture his lost colony. After the end of war he was appointed governor of the Bahamas, which became a refuge for many American loyalists, and served in the islands for a decade. In 1796 he was recalled home and retired to Ramsgate, Kent, where he died at the age of 78.

It is a testament to Kitty Blair's popularity and adeptness that she was quickly absorbed into the new social world of revolutionary Virginia after Dunmore fled Williamsburg in early June 1775. She remained friends with leading military officers and public officials of the new Commonwealth and remarried a few years later, leaving Virginia and moving south. We last see her in a delightful letter from Savannah, Georgia, in 1779. The letter provides only a tantalizing glimpse of her but sufficient to suggest that she remained as playful as ever, gaily unconcerned about her role in undermining Lord Dunmore and the British cause in America.

JAMES HORN
Vice President of Research
and Historical Interpretation,
The Colonial Williamsburg Foundation

A Cock and Bull for Kitty

> The evidence was voluminous and indecent.
> That of the defendant tended to prove on the
> Complainant original hatred, ill-temper,
> disobedience, refusal of conjugal rights,
> departure not without some hint of adultery,
> that of the complainant to fix on Dr. Blair
> impotence and hidden causes of disgust,
> and it was difficult to say on which side the
> evidence preponderated.[1]
>
> Thomas Jefferson

Word of the death of Lord Botetourt, the fourteenth crown governor of Virginia, reached Lord Hillsborough, the Secretary for Colonial Affairs, sometime in November of 1770.[2] Within a month, George III had named a successor and official notice was on its way to America: He was to be John Murray, Lord Dunmore, the 40-year-old Scotsman who was currently governor of New York.[3]

A member of the House of Lords since 1761, his Lordship was already on record as to how to govern Americans: "if left to themselves [they] would soon be quiet," he said.[4] Dunmore's comments were made during the Lords' debate over George III's annual speech on the state of the American colonies and immediately after a caution from Lord Chatham as to "how we invade the liberties of our fellow subjects." But Dunmore might also have been talking about the art of governing

Virginia, an art so expertly mastered by his predecessor, Botetourt, that under him Virginia's government was said to "almost execute itself."[5] Dunmore was never very good at doing what he preached. But perhaps the worst thing about having to succeed Botetourt in Virginia was that from the very beginning he found himself vying with a saint who made everything he did seem tainted – or worse.

As the situation in Virginia was critical – so critical that Dunmore's instructions were preparing with all possible dispatch – it was expected that he would go there at once.[6] Unhappily, Lord Dunmore did not want to go to Virginia. He wanted to remain in New York. As he would later put it, Virginia's unhealthy climate "will oblige me to live without my family, which will make my residence in that country, where there is little or no society . . . tiresome."[7] In short, he was not sure he would "be able to stay [in Virginia] any time, and therefore it might be more advantageous for me as well as my family that I should remain in [New York] where there is a harmony between me and the people . . .[which] at the same time suits so well with my disposition." It was a point he would make repeatedly in his letters to Lord Hillsborough and the Ministry: though he was told that it "was the King's pleasure that he lose no time in repairing to [Virginia],"[8] he simply could "not foresee anything . . . interrupt[ing] the design I had in coming to this country at first."[9]

Though Dunmore's private reply to Hillsborough's letter notifying him of his transfer has been lost, we can guess its contents from what he said in his letter of June 4, 1771.[10] In a word, he was still "inclined" toward New York.[11] Virginia's deadly agues were one reason. Another was the fees he received for issuing land patents, a valuable emolument of his office. Dunmore had already collected £14,248 in fees for issuing patents in New York – an extremely large sum for a royal governor who had only been in office nine months.[12] As the King had prohibited the issuance of new patents in the west, that door was now barred to him. His Lordship's dutiful subjects, the people of New York, received news of his transfer on March 4. Even then, Dunmore continued to use all his weight at home to remain in New York, including telling his brother-in-law and chief advocate at court, Earl Gower, that Virginia was sure to ruin his wife's health.[13]

Wheedling – repeating his wishes until he got his way – was typical of Dunmore. It was the behavior of a child, endearing to a mother, but probably not to the King of England. At least as jejune was Dunmore's June 4, 1771 suggestion that the man named to replace him in New York, Lt. Gov. William Tryon of North Carolina, should simply be sent to Virginia instead. "There can be no doubt that Mr. Tryon would be pleased with the exchange," he told Hillsborough, forgetting that in arguing for Virginia he was weakening the case for New York. "[A] stranger to both countries [he said] . . . cannot have a reason for choosing other than that which is esteemed the most advantageous as to emolument, and I am persuaded he will be equally agreeable to the people." So sure was Dunmore that he had found the right solution for everyone that he told Hillsborough he had now decided not to "remove from New York until he had a definite answer" to his proposal – which is to say he had gone from merely pleading his case to declaring the entire question moot. This too was typical of Dunmore: after cajolery, his favorite mode of persuasion was the artful *fait accompli*.[14]

Having at least convinced himself, he then went off on a boat trip to New Jersey. He was still there on July 7 when he got the news that Tryon and his wife had arrived in New York. To say that Dunmore was shocked by this development barely begins to express it: he was outraged.

At once, he called for a boat and set off for Paulus Hook.

From there, he took an oyster boat out to the Tryons' sloop, *Sukey*, where he half invited, half ordered them to join him for dinner at Fort George. William Smith, a member of the New York Governor's Council, came upon them shortly after their arrival.

He found the two governors "walking the Room & reading . . . Newpaper[s]" while Lady Tryon, who was both ill and exhausted from the trip, sat "neglected in a Couch or Sopha."[15] Whether this scene was enacted before Dunmore "warmly solicited" his successor "to make an Exchange" (in Tryon's words) or after perhaps does not matter. Tryon refused to be persuaded. "[I] could not with any possible Color of Decency retreat from a Province to which I was appointed to Preside over," he later explained to Lord Hillsborough. Besides, he and his wife were so fatigued they could not think of going to Virginia without first going to England to recover their health. The next day, Tryon took the oath of office, after which he and the colony's still seething former governor went off to New York's Town Hall for a public reading of Tryon's commission followed by a party.[16]

In his August 31 letter to Lord Hillsborough (quoted above), Tryon said nothing about Dunmore's outrageous conduct at the celebration following the swearing-in ceremony.[17] It may be that he took pity on Dunmore; more likely, he doubted whether he would be believed. It seems that his Lordship had gotten drunk, "called Tryon a Coward who had never seen Flanders," then careered about in the Night assaulting his guests, one of whom was a General Court judge. Dunmore capped off the evening by bawling, "Damn Virginia – Did I ever seek it? Why is it forced upon me? I askd for New York – New York I took, & they have robbed me of it without my Consent."[18]

It would be ninety days before Hillsborough replied to Dunmore's letter of June 4. Though Tryon was now firmly in place,

Dunmore continued to behave as if he were governor: continued to issue patents; continued to collect fees, albeit under very doubtful authority. For some time he had had his eye on a fine 51,000 acre plot on the shores of Lake Champlain. Unfortunately, he was prohibited from making individual grants of land in excess of 1,000 acres. But suppose he were to issue fifty-one grants of 1,000 acres each to fifty-one different individuals? And suppose those individuals, faced with offers they could not refuse, should sell to him? What possible objection could there be to that? More to the point, who was to know? So it happened that on July 12, 1771 fifty-one souls, friends of Dunmore all, sold fifty-one 1,000-acre plots of land to his Lordship for the mere "sum of five shillings to each of them in hand paid." What he would later call "a fair open and strictly legal acquisition" was only one of a series of fraudulent transactions that was to mark his career as governor in both New York and Virginia. This agreeable business accomplished, Dunmore then left for a hunting trip in western New York – but not before once again telling friends in New York that he had no intention of reporting to Virginia.[19]

"We know nothing as yet of our new Governor's coming amongst us" wrote the Virginia planter, Col. Richard Bland, to a merchant friend in London on August 1, 1771. "Sometimes it is said he will come, at other times that he will not. We entertain a very unfavorable opinion of him from the accounts brought to us from New York."[20] With that, Col. Bland passed on an account given to him by James Wood, a Virginia Assembly member "just returned from [New York]":

His Lordship, with a set of his drunken companions, sallied about midnight from his Palace, and attacked [New York] Chief Justice Horsmanden's coach & horses. The coach was destroyed & the poor horses lost their tails. The next day the Chief Justice applied to Government for redress, and a proclamation was issued by advice of the Council, offering a reward of 200 [pounds] for a discovery of the principal in this violent act. We have not heard whether the governor demanded the reward.[21]

Col. Bland's tone was arch, if not sarcastic, as befitted a prank that bore some resemblance to the "the rape" of Belinda's lock in Alexander Pope's eponymous poem. But Daniel Horsmanden (whose name may have inspired the act) was no mere figure of fun. An associate justice of the New York Supreme Court since 1737, and its chief justice since 1755, Horsmanden was well known in Virginia as the cousin of Council member William Byrd III.[22] As a result, his Lordship's escapade was sure to be not only widely-reported but widely-credited in Virginia.

Meanwhile, Virginia Acting Governor William Nelson had written Hillsborough on July 1, 1771 to say that he had heard from Lord Dunmore, but "nothing about . . . Virginia."[23] On July 11, Nelson appeared before the Virginia Assembly. His topic was the virtue of Botetourt and the receding hope that his successor would be "equally entitled to our . . affectionate Esteem."[24] In a reply suggestive of a Greek chorus, the Council praised Gov. Nelson's attention to the affairs of the colony office while deploring Botetourt's loss "in the strongest Manner." There was no mention of his successor:

> The many and great Virtues of our late worthy Governor, the Right Honourable Lord Botetourt, call upon us in the strongest Manner to condole with you on the Death of that noble Lord, who made the real Happiness of this colony, the Object of his most ardent Wishes. At the same time permit us, Sir, to express our Satisfaction in the great

Attention you have paid to the Affairs of Government
since the Administration devolved upon you, and to assure
you we think our Country happy in having a Native of your
distinguished Abilities and long Experience in Business to
preside over us.[25]

The House of Burgesses seconded the Council with a suitably
"Humble Address" of their own.[26] The entire Assembly then
took up and passed a much-needed flood relief bill. As there
was still no sign of Dunmore, Nelson ended the session. The
burgesses, planters all, returned to their fields. It was summer,
the "Dangerous Time," when Virginia's death rate from disease
was highest. For sixty-six days, Virginia waited. All correspondence between London, Dunmore and Nelson ceased.

Then, suddenly, on the morning of 25 September, Dunmore
rode into Williamsburg. He came on horseback, riding down
through New Jersey, Philadelphia and the Eastern Shores of
Maryland and Virginia to Yorktown escorted by his dogsbody,
Capt. Edward Foy, and an eleven-year-old boy, John Skey
Eustace, whose pretty sister Catherine ("Kitty") was rumored
to be his Lordship's mistress.[27]

As the Assembly was not in session, Dunmore had to be sat-
isfied with an indifferent greeting from a very mixed group of
local worthies. Still haunted by Lord Botetourt's "unwearied
attention to every duty of his exalted station, the easiness of
access to his person . . . [his] continual endeavors to reconcile . .
. the differences subsisting between Great Britain and her
colonies, and unremitted study to promote . . . prosperity," the
reception committee could think of no better way to salute their
new governor than to invoke the memory of the "worthy and
truly excellent" paragon he had been appointed to replace. It
was more a sigh of regret than a salutation; less a welcome than
an omen of trouble to come. (In case he missed the point,

Dunmore was told Botetourt's "great loss" could *never* be reme-
died.) Sadly, it all fell on a deaf ear. Instead of soothing noises of
commiseration, Dunmore offered "diffidence in [his]. . . abilities" and excuses for his delay so at odds with well known fact
as to be laughable.[28]

For those in Dunmore's audience interested in his success
(still a majority of those present), his failure to join in the general tribute to Botetourt was at least vaguely disconcerting.
Others, put off by rumors and his expressed diffidence, took
him at his word: he lacked abilities. This was a bad start, even
for a governor with a track record of success. Dunmore could
hardly be blamed for being put off by Virginians' idolatry of
Lord Botetourt. Virginians, their ears cauliflowered by rumors,
could be excused for viewing Dunmore as the *reductio ad absur-
dum* of the British imperium: "In stature he was low [one of
them later said], and though muscular and healthful he bore on
his head hoary symptoms of probably a greater age than he had
reached. To external accomplishments he pretended not, and
his manners and sentiments did not surpass substantial barbarism, a barbarism which was not palliated by a particle of
native genius nor regulated by one ingredient of religion. His
propensities were coarse and depraved."[29] Richard Henry Lee,
a future signer of the Declaration of Independence, would
later joke, "If [the Ministry] . . . had searched thro' the world
for a person best fitted to ruin their cause, and procure union
and success for these Colonies, they could not have found a
more complete Agent than Lord Dunmore."[30]

To this day, Dunmore continues to play the villain to Botetourt's saint in Williamsburg. But what is missing from carica-
tures of Dunmore is not just a little of the good to go with the
bad – oafish and crass though he may have been, Dunmore was
not without virtue, humanity or insight – it is some sense of how
his many defects loaned credence to the Whig fable of British

tyranny. Perhaps that is why the story of Dunmore's affair with pretty Kitty Eustace Blair, the scandal that his Lordship said "must destroy the happiness of his administration" if it was true, is so important. It *was* true – or at least believed to be. Worse, Dunmore then attempted to deny it "on his honor" – only to have to rescue that honor with a ploy so outrageous that it instantly transformed rumor into established fact.[31]

Kitty Eustace was the 19-year-old daughter of Dr. John Eustace of New York, who left his wife and children in 1764 or 65 to go live in Wilmington, North Carolina.[32] Whatever reason Eustace may have had for abandoning his family it had nothing to do with Dunmore, who did not arrive in New York until September 25, 1770, five years after Dr. Eustace's departure. Nor do we know how his wife and children came to be acquainted with his Lordship, only that it would be natural for them to seek an introduction to the colony's new governor, and that within the space of one year Dunmore was feeling so obliged to Kitty and her family that he agreed to pay the entire cost of John Skey Eustace's education at the College of William and Mary.[33]

Meanwhile, Dr. Eustace was experiencing a kind of rebirth in Wilmington where he was valued as much for his enjoyment of life and literature as for his skill as a physician. Variously described as a region in which "hospitality [was] carried to the extreme" and as a place of "general ease and prosperity . . . highly favorable to the cultivation of polite literature," Wilmington was perhaps most notable for its Cape Fear Library Society, a sort of combination lending library and literary society not unlike the famous Literary Club of Dr. Samuel Johnson.[34] As one of Wilmington's leading lights, as a man of "wit. . . genius. . . learning, and science," John Eustace would later be remembered primarily as the "correspondent of Lawrence Sterne,"[35] author of the famously indecent comic novel, *The Life and*

Opinions of Tristram Shandy, Gentleman (1759).[36] Whether Dr. Eustace succumbed to the area's extreme hospitality or a transient ague is unclear. What is certain is that he died in 1769; that his estate was probated in September of that year by his 36-year-old wife Margaret; and that when mother and daughter returned to New York in December they were carrying with them the heart and soul of Dr. Eustace's extensive collection of Eighteenth Century novels.

Norfolk being on the way from Wilmington to New York, the Eustace ladies decided to stop over at the home of their kinsman, local merchant Dr. Archibald Campbell.[37] Having liked what they saw of Norfolk, they returned in 1770, apparently to stay. Exactly when they met Norfolk merchant James Parker is unknown – only that Parker was so taken with Kitty that he began to feature her in his letters to his London associate Charles Steuart:[38]

> Kitty Eustace, the chip which you forwarded to this country, is to be married immediately after the General Court to Doctor Blair. There's a club of all our women out at Kemp's Landing fixing the riggin'. I think the doctor will marry more than one, not that I entertain a thought of Kitty's being concerned in any contraband trade, but the mother and her must go together. She's a clever managing sort of lady and has played her cards exceeding well.[39]

Though he knew that Margaret's maiden name was Campbell, Parker may not have known that she was the daughter of Laughlin Campbell, a wealthy Scotsman from the Isle of Islay who had been promised 100,000 acres of land in return for settling eighty-three families on the Hudson River. It was a promise New York Governor W.E. Cosby had no authority to make and though the New York Assembly did finally award Margaret and her five siblings 10,000 acres, she continued to tell friends that she was "oppressively kept from the possession of [lands] of great value."[40]

The young man who was fated to become Kitty's husband (and Dunmore's cuckold), Dr. James Blair, was the youngest son of John Blair Sr., president of the Virginia Council and twice (as a result of the deaths of former governors[41]) acting governor of Virginia. Like his friend Dr. Arthur Lee, James was a graduate of Edinburgh University medical school. Like Arthur Lee too, he had temporarily set aside medicine for a career as a political essayist. "The Doctors LEE and BLAIR are both here," wrote a London correspondent to Rind's *Gazette*, "and really do honour to Virginia by exerting themselves indefatigably in behalf of their country." The letter was dated March 16, 1769. Less than nine months later, Lee wrote James' father to say that his son had been "seiz'd six or seven days ago with a violent nervous disorder that effects the brain and every part of his body. I know not what the Physicians call it, but he now lays very ill." On his doctor's advice, James had tried the waters at Bath, to no avail. By October he was en route to Virginia, a trip Arthur Lee endorsed, as James seemed rather low. "[Y]ou must exert yourself," Lee chided his friend in a farewell letter, "& banish all gloomy ideas."[42]

Exactly when James Blair met Kitty and her mother is unknown. We do know that young Blair arrived in Norfolk on the ship *Fairfield* on November 29, 1770, and that he and Kitty were married on May 21, 1771 in Williamsburg's Bruton Parish Church and put to bed that night in the Blair family home at the west end of Duke of Gloucester Street – only to separate before morning. The would-be bridegroom never did say what happened that night, or if he did it was not recorded.[43] Neither did his would-be wife. But if James thought that Kitty would accept a quiet separation, he was wrong. Acting on the advice of her lawyer-manqué mother[44] and having told her husband's sister

The John Blair House
"Finding herself deserted, Kitty removed not 100 paces off"

Ann Blair that "nothing shall tempt me to take upon myself a Guilt my heart does not accuse me of," Kitty had every intention of airing her grievance in court.[45]

Blair v. Blair, the case that was to make prophets of Dunmore's worst enemies, was a cause célèbre from the start. It had it all: money, weird sex and a taint of corruption. As a family of respected lawyers, teachers and clergymen, the Blairs were as influential as they were rich: not the first family in Virginia perhaps, but certainly among the leading forty. Between awe of them and allure of Kitty, there was easily enough to attract a lawyer, and the lawyers attracted to the case, initially a claim for alimony, were among Virginia's best. Appearing for Kitty was the legal odd couple of Attorney General John Randolph and Patrick Henry, colonial Virginia's most ardent Anglophile and its fieriest King baiter. Representing her husband, Dr. James Blair, and, following the doctor's death, his estate, were Edmund Pendleton (the Cicero of the Virginia bar), James Mercer (its best pure advocate), College of William and Mary law professor George Wythe and his star pupil, Thomas Jefferson. The authorities called in aid were equally grand: Jefferson's brief for James Blair quoted liberally from the *Bible*, John

Milton, John Locke and Montaigne, as well as Mosaic, Roman and Greek law – all enlivened by occasional references to the "Custom of Amazons to copulate . . . at certain times."[46] But what gave the case its perverse stature and significance was that the "other man" was not only Governor of the colony, but Chief Judge of the court in which the case would be decided. In short, it promised to be a good show from beginning to end and, with Dunmore presiding, a feast for gossips.

Following established practice, Kitty's lawsuit was styled as an action for alimony. But should her claim for alimony fail for lack of a properly consummated marriage, she prayed for maintenance on an implied contract, which is to say a contract imposed by the court. To no one's surprise, James's answer was a mirror image of Kitty's complaint and prayer for relief: as it was clear that the marriage had never been consummated, Kitty could not qualify for alimony. As James had not agreed in writing to pay maintenance, he could not be forced to do so by a judge. Should it, however, be decided that Kitty was his legal wife (under the law, the most likely result), James wanted a divorce but without an order to pay alimony, Kitty having failed in her wifely duty. The problem with this strategy was that divorce was illegal in Virginia except by act of the Assembly, and though James's lawyers believed the Assembly had the power to pass such a law, Thomas Jefferson (who did the legal research) was unable to find any such law in the statute books. A further complication was Kitty's age. She was not yet 21. Accordingly, her case was brought in the name of her "next friend," Margaret, a quaint legalism that added the authority of a trustee to the influence of a mother so totally in agreement with her daughter's wishes that the "two must go together."[47]

Not to be neglected was the factual question of whether the failure of the marriage was due to Dr. Blair, to whom James

Parker assigned a perplexing variety of "different instruments" or his would-be wife whose "thing" (another Parker euphemism) was said to lack "capacity."[48] In short, the Blairs' marital plight quickly became the subject of intense speculation by gossips seeking to reconcile Kitty's supposed lack of capacity with her randy earl's voracious sexual appetite. For James, it would come down to "neither more nor less than a question concerning my virility."[49] For Margaret, who was well off but not rich and had hoped Blair family wealth and connections would set her up for life, James's inability to perform was as troubling as it was unexpected. Should he die – and he remained quite sickly – Kitty would be left with nothing. Nor was Margaret, a newcomer in "a Land of Strangers", likely to call upon connections of her own.[50]

The issues being fairly joined, it might be thought that sanity would prevail. It did not. Nor could a year of mediation untangle what was increasingly called "Kitty's Case."[51] Kitty, Margaret Eustace, Dr. Blair – all had yet to learn that justice is what people fashion for themselves.

By May 1772 it had become clear that only an act of congress – which is to say, a completed act of sexual intercourse – could make Kitty and James Blair a couple. So it happened that Dunmore (of all people) was asked to play the part of honest broker: everyone concerned, including Dr. Campbell, got an invitation to dinner at the palace, at which Kitty agreed "to let [James] make a push" at the end of General Court term in late May.[52] We are told that Dr. Campbell added a prudent counsel and that the two left seemingly reconciled. But whether it was terminal embarrassment – the fact that Dunmore was putting all his weight behind his push could not have helped – or terminal impotence, James's second effort proved no better than his first:

There's Nothing Yet done at Williamsburg in Kitty's Case

[Parker wrote on June 12, 1772.] We thought the matter was entirely Settled at the last Arbitration, but it Seems she jumped out of bed & would not do anything. I shall advise the next time I see him [James] to lay a Young Whore in the bed beside her that She may see that [which] he Requires of her. There never was such a piece of work. Her thing is talked of all over the Country.[53]

Though Parker chose to pass in silence over the spectacle of Lord Dunmore trying to rouse his cuckold to his marital duty by pimping for his wife, we can be sure that local Whigs did not.

As it turned out, Kitty's problem had little to do with the terms of her Dunmore brokered reconciliation and even less to do with having to be shown what was required of her. An anonymous letter had "fallen" (as she put it) into her hands on the day after the Palace dinner. [54] The letter said only "I have believed & Experience will confirm it that Dr. Blair is incompetent", [55] but that was enough, as she told James's sister Ann on July 18, 1772, to "blast . . . [her] every sanguine wish":

The little pains your Brother took to be ascertained of my Affection before Marriage, is too well known to you all and as I knew it was perfectly agreeable to the best of parents, & that I loved & valued your family one and all of them, at the same time no particular Objection to your Brother – nor no partiality in Favor of any other person in my mind – I had no reason to doubt that Gratitude and Esteem for the Affection he had for me would enable me to discharge the most rigid Duties of a good wife – when that accursed Letter which fell into my hands the evening after blasted every sanguine wish of your friend. [56]

"Forgive me [she continued] when I tell you there were too

A Cock and Bull for Kitty

many Circums[tance]s in y[ou]r Br[other]'s Manner of Conduct, that seem'd a Confirm[atio]n of the Charge a[gains]t him wh[ich] chased from my Heart that Esteem I shou'd otherwise have felt for him."[57] There it was: no lack of wifely duty, only a surfeit of wifely disgust for a husband who failed to behave as a husband should.

Clearly, Kitty had talked herself into marriage. She even described the process: she had married because she valued her husband's family. She loved him because he loved *her*. Even her gratitude was suspect, being derived from her respect for James's affection for her. This was self love masquerading as love of James – but without the prospect of a fusion of respect and fondness over a lifetime, as there would be in the case of George and Martha Washington. In agreeing to discharge the most rigid duties of a wife, Kitty was simply making the best of a bad bargain.

It was not surprising, given her views on marriage, that Kitty resented her husband. It was *he* who had failed to note her lack of affection; *he* whose gestures had confirmed her worst fears. That said, his conduct toward her since the marriage had been so "uniformly tender" that she had "resolved . . . to cherish every grateful Thought . . . til her heart was softened." Having talked herself out of marriage, she now tried to talk herself back in. As she told Ann,

The Time is now arrived in which I can assure you with Truth, that your Brother nor any of his Family shall have no just Cause to complain of me for the future and [there is] nothing I more ardently wish than an affectionate Embrace from one & all of them which will be most sincerely return'd by me.[58]

It sounded like surrender. But if Ann thought that she was even more deluded than her brother. "I have as much

30

Sensibility as your Brother [Kitty went on] and . . . suffered as much & deserved it as little. I have received Indignities I would not. . . inflict . . . from cruel and hard hearted strangers. But notwithstanding, I have as many Testimonies of worthy Hearts bleeding for my Distress as he can boast and nothing shall tempt me to take upon myself a Guilt my Heart does not accuse me of." Until now, Kitty had not divulged the reason for her conduct, but if were the case to go to trial, Anne would find that she was not without "some Excuse" in the eyes of the world.

It was a threat and, under the circumstances, a serious one. Kitty would tell all. The grotesque particulars of her marriage would be transformed into a test of popularity, one which the Blairs might lose in a colony grown tired of special favors for "Great needy Ones."[59] She did not say that Lord Dunmore was ready to leap to her defense. But then she did not need to. As a recent visitor to Virginia had noted, a system which allowed judges "to sit one hour and hear a cause as a court of law and the next hour, perhaps minute, to sit and hear the cause as a court of . . . equity" was all too likely to give "directly contrary decisions" with "mischievous consequences."[60] This was certainly no less true where the judge was enjoying the favors of one of the parties before the court. Nor did Kitty need to remind her sister-in-law that she had two of the best lawyers in Virginia. But surely it was Kitty's letter that spoke loudest to Ann: this was not the language of feminine submission.

Here was a woman who took strength from adversity; who espoused an elegant prose style as much for its transformative power as its social cachet. At a time when the spelling of socially advantaged ladies like Abigail Adams and Martha Washington was at its best unreliable, Kitty Eustace's orthography was as good as a pedigree. Granting that many of her phrases could be traced to books in her father's library, (with "accursed letter" and "sanguine wish" from Smollett's *Peregrine Pickle* leading the list); granting also that her view of herself as a swooning victim of cruel and hard-hearted strangers was somewhat belied by her staunch refusal to admit to guilt contrary to her heart, Kitty was as well read as any woman in Virginia – including Ann. Nor did she lack for more cerebral models, her father's library having introduced her to skeptics (David Hume), cynics (Jonathan Swift) and anonymous misogynists (*The Woman Hater*). Having been deserted by her father at the age of twelve, she might have hated all men on principle. Instead, she had interposed "the best of mothers" (from *Tom Jones*), affected the *Pamela* heroine-in-distress (from Samuel Richardson's eponymous novel) and gone in search of worthier hearts. As she told Ann, she had as much sensibility as anyone. All that she lacked was a proper object.[61]

In his 1768 letter to Lawrence Sterne, Dr. Eustace had spoken of his admiration for the novelist's ability to "frisk and curvet with ease through . . . intricacies of sentiment." "It is not always possible for everyone to taste humor," Sterne had cautioned in his reply. He then went on to characterize the doctor as a "true feeler," someone he was proud to have on "his side . . . from the beginning" as he "always brings half the entertainment along with him." "[H]is own ideas [Sterne added] are only call'd forth by what he reads, and the vibrations within, so entirely do they correspond with those excited, 'tis like reading *himself* and not the book." It was, in the language of the day, a noble compliment – one that Dr. Eustace decided to share with members of the Cape Fear Library Society, hoping perhaps that it might one day become his epitaph, as indeed it has by dint of frequent quotation in scholarly introductions to *Tristram Shandy*.

Like her father, Kitty was a true feeler; someone who brought half the fun with her; someone capable, in the words of

Charles Dickens, of being the heroine of her own life. A "fallen woman" by the standards of a later era, Kitty might today be called a "proto feminist," neither of which phrase comes close to capturing her fierce *joie de vivre* or her allure for men. It is easy to see why Kitty was so disgusted by her first encounter with the marital pallet. Where was the thrill? The pure fusion of souls? The worthy hearts bleeding for her distress? Was she, the mistress of an Earl, to be reduced to a mere "good wife"? She might not be blameless, but neither would she be tempted to feel a guilt so contrary to her heart. That was what she had told Ann Blair, in a sentence that might have been written by Lawrence Sterne himself, so little did it depend on conventional ideas of marriage.

While Kitty was "resolv[ing] . . . to cherish every Grateful thought" on the theme of marriage, her mother was trying to decide what to do about the anonymous letter. One thing she did was to show it to her friends. Among these, one of the first to see it was her lodger, St. George Tucker, a William and Mary law student and cousin to Dr. Archibald Campbell. At age twenty, Tucker was young; too young to know that he should steer clear of such scandals. Perhaps he felt flattered to be taken for a real lawyer. Perhaps he was in love with Kitty himself – or just being kind to a fellow stranger to Virginia. Be that as it may, Tucker gave Margaret some good advice: dismiss the letter as the work of a meddler.

That was easy to say, not so easy to do. Deprived of her share of 100,000 acres, denied the dignity owed to her as the daughter of a kinsman to the Duke of Argyle, Margaret Eustace was in no mood – or condition – to endure another miscarriage of justice. She had worked hard to get Kitty a place in Virginia society, a goal her daughter clearly endorsed. Nor could she afford to ignore the legal issues raised by Blair's failure to perform: Was Kitty legally married or not? If she was not married, how would she support herself? And if she was, what was the status of her own property, presumed by law to now belong to her husband?[62]

In any case, Margaret did not dismiss the letter. She showed it to Dr. Campbell and James's sister Ann (who may or may not have mentioned it to her brother.) It was not long before the people of Williamsburg were once again hearing about James's instruments including, evidently, Blair himself who wrote his would-be mother-in-law on 18 September 1772 to demand the names of everyone who had either been shown the letter or informed of its contents. In her reply, dated the 20th, Margaret denied making a confidant of anyone but Ann Blair and Dr.

St. George Tucker
"Flattered to be
taken for a real
lawyer"

Campbell "who you yourself first informed long before I was acquainted with your sentiments." Candid to a fault, Margaret also admitted to frequent conversations with St. George Tucker. But that was only after the law student had already received "his first intelligence f[ro]m the world." "[A]fter them both [meaning, Ann and Tucker] let Dr. Campbell too produce my Letters," she said. Dr. Blair then wrote to Tucker, quoting from Margaret's letter and saying, "I presume that I am to ask you what passed in the frequent Conversations you have had with Mrs. Eustace relative to the odious Subject."[63]

When he got James's letter, Tucker's career must have passed in front of his eyes. His legal advice to Margaret Eustace was about to make him famous before he was even known. His first appearance in court would not be as a bewigged lawyer, but as a witness in a lawsuit over the nature of a gentleman's instruments and the capacity of a young lady's thing. Tucker took his time before replying, apparently to seek counsel from his mentor, Rev. Thomas Gwatkin, administrator of the Grammar School at the College of William and Mary. Meanwhile, Kitty had asked Tucker to make a copy of the letter for her husband. Fearing that his handwritten copy might implicate him in the authorship of the original, Tucker told her to ask someone else. But that was only after asking Prof. Gwatkin to make a copy. (No fool, Gwatkin said "No.") After huddling with Kitty, Tucker wrote to James on September 20, offering to answer James's request for information by quoting at length from the letter –which he then did, temporarily putting an end to any talk of marital pushes and reunions.

Two months passed. Fall Public Time, when the population of Williamsburg swelled from 1,800 to 6,000 and most of the colony's business was transacted, came and went. For the first time since his arrival in 1771, Dunmore was the subject of genuine affection. "I think I discover many Good Qualities in him," wrote William Nelson Sr., speaking for many, including George Washington who never came down to Williamsburg without taking dinner at the Palace or joining Dunmore for a play at the theater behind the Capitol (Washington's treat.)[64] An observer would later recall that "socially the little principality reached its full flower in Lord Dunmore's second year," adding, "The palace was thronged with charming inmates and guests."[65] So much the worse then, that his Lordship's golden age should be destroyed by what James Parker called "a very foolish letter" from Dr. Blair, accusing the governor of having an affair with Kitty. The letter is now lost. Happily for us, James Parker described the contents of the letter in some detail:

Matters are now come to an open rupture at Williamsburg. A suit is commenced by Mrs. B[lair] for a separate maintenance. As to the goodness of the blood, I'm in no doubt at all about it, but in this case, I fancy the fault will turn out on the other side. The Dr. wrote a very foolish letter to Ld.

D[unmo]r[e] on the subject, who sent for his brother John and laid it before him, assured him upon his honor that had he ever inclined to such a connection that disturbing the peace of the Blair family and their friends would have totally destroyed his peace and render him unhappy in his government. At the same time [he] desired [John Blair] to inform the Dr. that if he did not retract what he had wrote, he [John Blair] must lay aside the governor. The Dr. I understand has made concessions to Capt. Foy. So the matter stands. The old lady persists her daughter is still a maid, and that the Dr. never has and indeed cannot do as a man should do. For my own part, I was once of the side that blamed Kitty. I have now altered my opinion. As to the Governor I don't believe he ever had any such intention. The old woman says she has wrote a state of the case and talks of publishing it. Let them work out their own salvation. I am determined to keep clear. I was once asked to be upon the arbitration.[66]

His Lordship had not denied adultery; he simply rephrased the question. If there was a connection, it was a distant one, as in *"such a* connection" – never a capital "C," *"CONNECTION."* The problem with arguments in the subjunctive, a problem Dunmore never seemed to grasp, is that "if" assumes the existence of the fact at issue. In a town teeming with salacious rumors, many of them having to do with Dunmore himself, an assumed fact was as good as a proven one. His ability to govern a people who looked to Botetourt as a model of decorum would be lost. Loyalists like James Parker might stand with him, but sober men like Col. Bland would not. Nor was Dunmore likely to convince Whigs like Richard Henry Lee with assurances based on his honor.

An innocent man might simply have asked for a retraction.

Instead, Dunmore threatened Dr. Blair's brother John, as family head, with the loss of his patronage, a threat in keeping with his idea of honor but quite at odds with Virginia notions of propriety. James was promptly sent over to the Palace to offer concessions. But apologies to Capt. Foy failed to reach the core of Dunmore's dilemma: how to extricate himself from a scandal without doing injury to his mistress. Then, suddenly, on December 30, 1772, James Blair died. Parker, writing to Charles Steuart in February, thought it would help Kitty: "Doctor Blair has very opportunely taken his departure for the other world, by which 'tis to be hoped Kitty's case will be helped. She will get his dowry at all events."[67] Parker was right. James's death transformed a problematic claim into a viable one. The alimony-seeking estranged wife was no more. Enter the widow, with a widow's right to one half of Dr. Blair's estate. Legally, Kitty's claim still required a valid marriage, but the burden of proof had shifted. The Blairs would now have to prove that the marriage was *in*valid, a difficult burden given the legal presumption in favor of marriage. What had begun as a lawsuit without law was settling into a *prima facie* case of liability for the estate. It was time to talk.

Whether the parties did in fact talk is unclear. On May 19, 1773 Parker wrote, "[The Blairs still "Refuse to give [Kitty] her dower, There is a Suit for it in James City Court, I do not see upon what principle they withhold it from her. I think 'twd be best to give them Something and let them de Camp."[68] We need not speculate whether Lord Dunmore was in agreement with this view. Unfortunately, he had more than enough on his hands already, dealing with another salacious rumor – only this time it was not Kitty but John Randolph's 18 year-old daughter, "Sukey" (Susannah), described by a British officer who saw her in 1774 as one of the "two greatest beautys in America."[69] The rumor was detailed by Parker in a oblique coda to his May 19 letter to Charles Steuart: "There's terrible [sex][70] stories at Wmsbg about the G & the Aty's daughter Sukey, & what is worst they Say Jack & the Mother know all about it, but [he will] pay for his fun there, if I'm not greatly mistaken. Indeed he has paid and is Security for Something considerable already. Not a word of this, God bless you, to any created thing. I've always considered Jack as a D[amne]d Villain."[71] Titillating though it might be to Parker and Steuart, the rumor was implausible on its face. Not even Dunmore would dare seduce the daughter of his own Attorney General, nor would Randolph have permitted it, let alone taken money for it, with all that might imply. As salacious rumors go, however, it is a fair indication of just how disliked both men were.

Blair v. Blair, now an action to enforce Kitty's right of dower, finally went to trial in James City Courthouse on Market Square in the summer of 1773.[72] The county court judge found in favor of the estate, whereupon Margaret took an appeal to General Court, Chief Judge Dunmore presiding. According to James Parker, "The principal evidences [were], Kitty's mother; contra, Mrs. Blair, the widow of Chowder, a Hardiman by birth and [a] full blooded [Virginia aristocrat]. 'Tis said the ladies were very liberal of their compliments to each other and talked a great deal of [sex]. [Kitty] gets a plantation and 16 Negroes during life, and about 600 [pounds] cash."[73] Certainly the General Court lost no time in finding for Kitty. It heard the arguments of counsel on the morning of November 3, 1773 and ruled that afternoon. The next day, Margaret passed the good news on to her friend, physician-poet, now lawyer Thomas Burke:

Yesterday *Day* Ever to be remembered with a greatfull Heart, my Dear Kitt's Law Suit was Determined in her favour with every Person of the Court But one the *professed Slave of Miss Blair* with Lord Dunmore at their

Head, in Spite of large Connections in a Land of
Strangers. Nothing, thanks to my good & merciful God –
no nothing let me repeat it again of allegations against Her.

The *Great* Pendleton abashed, Confused, in a State
remarked by all of almost total Stupefaction, & what he
Said so little to the purpose that he lost Credit as well as
Cause. Not so my Worthy friend [Patrick] Henry. He they
say Shind in the Cause of Justice Backed by the Law.

The Attorney General insisted on Opening the Cause.
He waited on Mr. Henry a few days before & told him he
had for Some time been preparing for it without Ever
Communicating one word to us on the Subject. He did So
in So masterly a manner that Every one Says He Out did
his usual Out Doings And pled to it four Hours then Seconded by Mr. Henry. Every Indifferent Spectator Seemed
to Demand by their looks a favourable Determination for
Kitty which was Soon given . . . . all is Settled respecting
Lands, Negroes, Money and the rest of the personal
Estate . . . .[74]

The parties were not permitted to introduce new evidence on
appeal, but there were more than enough references to female
things and male instruments in the record to give Margaret fits.
Despite the rumors, despite large family connections in a land
of strangers, Kitty had triumphed at last, in the process earning
redemption for both herself and her mother. Nor was it surprising that in her hour of victory Margaret should think of her
"land affairs" in New York: Burke was reminded of his promise to take legal action.[75] It was certainly an ending worthy of
Tristram Shandy, as true (in Sterne's phrase) to the "passions
[and]. . . ignorance or sensibility" of the age as it was to the
unique circumstances of Kitty's case.[76] With the Attorney
General out doing his usual outdoings and Patrick Henry in

full cry, it required (as Margaret said) only a few demanding looks from the spectators to ensure that justice was done.

Margaret chose to thank God that there was no mention of adultery by Kitty.[77] She would have done better to thank Dunmore. Having finally awakened to the dangers of his situation, he had worked behind the scenes to effect a synthesis of corruption and deceit unique even to himself.

If there was nothing odd about John Randolph (as senior lawyer) opening Kitty's case, that could not be said of his failure to inform his co-counsel of his plans until a few days before the hearing, particularly since Randolph had been preparing for some time. Nor did the prerogatives of a senior counsel – or attorney general – explain Randolph's *insistence*. That Randolph so monopolized the argument that Henry could only second him was also odd. Masterful though Randolph might be, it was Henry who was viewed as Virginia's foremost orator. The Attorney General had not only given his colleague no chance to speak; he left him with nothing to say. At the same time, Randolph had apparently failed to communicate one word of his strategy to his clients.

But by far the oddest part of the proceeding was Randolph's lack of concern over venturing so deeply into the den of the court's chief judicial lion, as shown by his remark that "Had the

General Court
"He outdid his usual outdoings"

defendant intended to object [to] adultery . . . he should have pleaded it . . . but this not having been done, it is to be hoped no insinuations will impress the ear of the court." This was not argument. This was an outright dare to the other side, and a dangerous one at that. Did Blair's lawyers have *proof* of adultery? Rumor said that they did. Well, let them produce it. And make it good. The court's "ear," Randolph declared impatiently, must not be defiled by idle gossip.[78]

Jefferson, whose case notes are our sole source for what was said in court, ascribed the failure to offer "suspicions of adultery" to the fact that the suspected adulterer in question was Dunmore. Only a fool – and Pendleton, Jefferson and Mercer were no fools – would impugn the chief judge. Randolph knew his Lordship's ear would be safe from blemish, even if the Blairs had proof. But (as lawyers like to say) that argument does not quite reach the issue. Dread of Lord Dunmore might explain the reluctance of the Blair family lawyers to *raise* the subject of adultery. But it did not explain Randolph's seeming recklessness in daring them to do so in the first place. The subject was too delicate, too explosive: Why imperil the peace of Virginia? Better yet, why would Randolph, a close personal friend of Lord Dunmore and a high official in his government – a man so desperate to make himself known to the nobility that he had used a condolence letter to Botetourt's nephew, the Duke of Beaufort, to claim a distant kinship with him – take that risk? There could only be one answer: *because Dunmore had asked him to do it*, knowing that opposing counsel could not afford to take his dare, knowing that their failure to do so would silence all rumors. With that, Randolph yielded his place at bar to Patrick Henry, scourge of tyrants. Left wholly in the dark as to the strategy, with nothing left to say on the law, it is not surprising that Henry chose (as Jefferson sneeringly put it) to "run wild in the field of fact."[79]

It was then left to Pendleton for the Blair family to make the best of a bad case. As Pendleton saw it, James's only error was to believe that Kitty had loved him, while Kitty, being "utterly determined against the nuptial rites" from the start, had failed to perform "a single condition . . . express or implied in the ceremonies of marriage." It was not only "impossible" for Kitty to seek "advantages from [Dr. Blair]," it was inequitable. None of this could be called law; even less could it be called argument. Pendleton clearly had a loser on his hands and he knew it. Still, he tried to put on a good show, dutifully reciting Jefferson's catalogue of the "Miscellaneous [sexual] Practices of several Nations," while flogging Puttendorf on "the moral obligation on Man to propagate" and Milton on marriage. Margaret Eustace was surely correct in describing him as "abashed," his stupefaction "total." Mercer had little to add. No trial lawyer and no orator, Jefferson was left with the job of note taker.[80]

Randolph could say that he had done himself and his country a great service. He had helped restore his Lordship's peace of mind and with it the happiness of his government. But if Randolph thought that, he was even more deluded than his friend. Even Dunmore could see that for a man who was hated, rumor was as good as fact. What he could not see was that he had given his enemies something more damaging than rumors of adultery: a case in point to show that the government of Virginia was in the hands of a tyrant. It was the kind of gaffe British Whigs like Edmund Burke had been warning about for years – enough, when added to Dunmore's other offenses, to perhaps give rise to demands for his recall. For the Whigs of Virginia, Dunmore's efforts in aid of Kitty were all too reminiscent of his lawsuit against his Lieutenant Governor in New York, a lawsuit brought in chancery court, in which Dunmore was *sole judge*![81]

For Kitty, *Blair v. Blair* was as much about money as about acceptance. While Margaret was touting her "Kitt's" victory, her daughter was marshaling her assets. *Blair v. Blair* was decided on November 3, 1773. Forty-seven days later, Kitty placed an ad in Purdie and Dixon's *Virginia Gazette* announcing a public auction of her one half interest in the "CATTLE, HOGS, PLANTATION UTENSILS" on Dr. Blair's plantation in Hanover County: "[A]t the same time and place [January 1, 1774] will be rented, to the best bidder, all my dower in the said Mr. Blair's lands and slaves; among the slaves there are five workers." The notice was signed simply "C. BLAIR" and included this post-script: "I also have a handy cook fellow to hire."[82]

Clearly, a lawyer – or perhaps a law student – had helped Kitty draft this ad.[83] Just as clearly, she was willing to be thought unfeeling in her haste to turn her cattle into cash. Except for the "p.s." (no doubt added by Kitty herself), her ad reads like other ads in the *Gazette*. Still, her postscript shows that Kitty was still Kitty, still the heroine of her own life, still bent on wringing the last penny from her ill-fated marriage. She drew no particular lesson from her experience; nor was she willing to alter her coquettish ways. Only a year later she would tell Thomas Burke that she had heard such flattering descriptions of his home in the North Carolina "Wilds" from his friend Munro that she was "thinking a clever fellow [i.e. Munro] might prevail on me to make one in your group." With that in mind, she had "applied to [Munro and another gentleman] . . . but they both Declined." Worse, it seemed that fellow Munro was "already caught [up] with some gypsy out [Burke's] way." Kitty's innuendo transformed sexual politics into insights into human nature: "[Y]ou know I told you I knew something of the theory of things in general [she told Burke] and you may tell [Munro] that the marks are upon him; so there's no hopes for me in that Quarter." The letter was dated November 18, 1774 and is the only letter of Kitty's to Burke to have survived. She signed it "C: Blair," coyly adding "how long I shall be distinguished by this name I can't Positively say."[84]

So it was that the true feelers prevailed. James's brother John, a later appointee to the U.S. Supreme Court, had a lawyer's bill to prove it. One might think that the bitterness of the contest would have made enemies of Kitty and the Blairs. It did not. In fact, in a March 13, 1777 letter to his sister Mary Braxton, John Blair described his "cousin Eustace" as a member of his family who often accompanied his wife as a companion.[85] "I was in hopes [he wrote] my wife would by this time have been with you, but poor Jeaney is so afflicted with hysterics (& my Cousin Eustace too is not well) that she cannot possibly leave home." Our last glimpse of Kitty in Williamsburg is at a Capitol ball in June 1777 – in the midst of war. According to an observer, she "made the best appearance as a Dancer." Who can doubt it?[86]

John Blair, Jr.
"A lawyer's bill to prove it"

For Lord Dunmore, the successful conclusion of *Blair* v. *Blair* marked both a personal victory and the beginning of his long slide into not-unmerited historical ignominy.

Jean Blair
"Poor Jeaney is afflicted with hysterics"

On June 8, 1775, less than two years after deciding Kitty's case, he "eloped" to a British frigate, claiming that he and his family had been threatened with injury by various unnamed Virginians.[87] He failed to say that at least some of those threats were the result of his seizure (on Ministry orders) of the colony's only store of gunpowder and his own threat to start a race war. For a year, he sailed up and down Chesapeake Bay, bombarding the homes of friends and enemies alike, making good on his threat to free and arm the slaves, even, it was alleged, putting Norfolk to the torch. Eventually, the King would lose all patience with his private war of revenge and recall him to Great Britain.

That Dunmore meant to inflict a race war on his former subjects is clear. What is not so clear, pending a fair-minded analysis of the evidence, is that he lacked cause. His freeing of the slaves was viewed as an atrocity by a paranoid, freedom-obsessed people. Now it might be viewed as the first truly meaningful effort to end slavery in British America. If it is wrong to say that Dunmore was a good man, it is just as wrong to say that he was all bad. As his many affidavits in the files of the Royal Commission on Loyalist Losses would suggest, he was truly tireless in supporting anyone who was loyal to him or to the British government.[88] He was also a fierce advocate for "quick dispatch" of his subjects' business affairs in London[89] and more than one historian has found "incontrovertible proof" of his "faithfulness . . . to the interests of . . . Virginians" in the records of his administration.[90] To be sure, his actions sometimes may have reminded Virginians of an episode from *Tom Jones*. But there was nothing funny about the final judgment. As Edmund Randolph later put it, Dunmore "was a man who preferred crooked ways to the direct way of winning the human heart, a pedant, a cynic, barbarous in manners and sentiment, lacking in genius, irreligious, coarse and depraved."[91] Randolph clearly knew whereof he spoke. His father was one of Dunmore's closest Virginia friends. In fact, his Lordship spent his last night in Williamsburg at the Randolph house plotting his escape. If anyone knew his true nature, it was surely the son of the man Parker called "that villain" Jack Randolph.[92]

It was as a judge that Lord Dunmore came closest to affirming the Whig case. Sexual hijinks by the nobility were tolerated in both Virginia and England. The problem arose when the rake was also a judge seeking to subvert the law to help his mistress. At that point, sexual hijinks could be assimilated to the failures of a colonial policy bereft of legitimacy. On November 3, 1773, the date Dunmore decided Kitty's case, Virginia was at a tipping point. The ensuing rebellion would be ascribed by the Whigs (and generations of scholars) to "tyranny" – a not entirely unfair characterization of Dunmore's record of malfeasance as a judge and governor. To be sure, Virginians were also influenced by the cycle of provocation and retaliation in Boston. Revolutions, like politics, are ultimately local, however, and the revolution in Virginia was so incomprehensible on its face that in 1775 Dr. Johnson would ask (in *Taxation No Tyranny*) "Why is it that the loudest yelps about liberty we hear come from the drivers of Negroes?" That he was falsely accused by Jefferson of burning Norfolk in the Declaration of Independence does not excuse Dunmore from wishing to make Virginians "feel . . . distress and misery," but it might inspire "a candid world" to revisit the idea that he was a chief cause of the Revolution in Virginia.[93]

Perhaps the best assessment of Dunmore as a governor and a man was given by a passing British officer whose 1774 visit to Williamsburg included dinner at the Governor's Palace. "His Lordship," Augustine Prevost wrote later, "is a jolly hearted companion . . . by no means bad . . .[in his] private character" but "the most unfit, most trifling and . . . uncalculated person living."[94] Indeed, the prevailing view of Dunmore in Virginia at the time was not hatred but disdain; not dread as of a tyrant, but exasperation, as with a deceitful, willful child. "Deviate, I conjure you, for once, into candour," cried "A Virginian" in Thomas Pinkney's June 29, 1775 *Virginia Gazette*. "To what fatality, my lord, can it be imputed that you, who have been hitherto considered as an inoffensive, easy, good natured man, should suddenly become black as the Ethiop, and prostitute abilities, never, indeed, designed to shine in the superior spheres of life, but which, in the calm retreats of social converse, if properly managed, might exempt you from censure?"[95] While Dunmore might not meet the Whig test of a tyrant, he easily met the common definition of an ass. In fact his Lordship was less ass than dupe, less a foe to American liberties than his own worst enemy.

But was it all true? Was Kitty Eustace Blair really Lord Dunmore's mistress? The evidence, though certainly circumstantial, is about as persuasive as such evidence can be. There seems to be no doubt, for example, that his Lordship had known the Eustaces in New York. What is more, he knew them well enough to pay the entire cost of educating John Skey Eustace out of his own pocket – a substantial investment, suggesting an equally substantial obligation of some kind to his family. Nor was that the end of Dunmore's generosity. When the war began, he sent young Eustace off to New York with his recommendation to Gen. Howe, commander in chief of the British army – a kindness John promptly repaid by betraying both his patron and his British officer escort to Gen. Washington.[96] While he was a bad enemy, Dunmore could be very generous to anyone willing to do his bidding.

Speaking circumstantially, the best evidence of the affair may be Augustine Prevost's diary: As someone unacquainted with either Dunmore or Williamsburg, Prevost was in no position to determine the truth of all the "scandalous rumors" he heard in the city's taverns. But he did have an after dinner tete-a-tete with Lady Dunmore ("a most agreeable pretty woman.") He later wrote, "His Lordship is I believe a consummate rake & does not pay that attention to his Lady that she seems to deserve. She is extremely jealous I am told of a young lady, whom it is reported was very dear to him previous to her Ladyship's arrival & the scandalous chronicle says his Lordship is very great there still." Prevost failed to note the name of the young lady in his diary.[97] The important thing however is that a stranger to Dunmore and Williamsburg should be greeted on his arrival with rumors about Dunmore's *continuing* affair with a young lady in Williamsburg and that he could not discount those rumors based on what he observed at his Lordship's dinner table. Was the young lady Kitty, Sukey Randolph, someone else – or all of them together? We may never know for sure.

In the end of course it does not matter. What matters is not whether Dunmore had an affair with Kitty Eustace Blair but whether the people of Virginia *believed* that he had – and whether these rumors were active on the political and social landscape of Virginia at a time when the case for American rights and liberties was being hotly debated in local newspapers. As Dunmore admitted, if the rumors were true it would destroy the happiness of his government. So it was that Jefferson's suspicions gained credence from rumors heard (and reported) by James Parker and Augustine Prevost, until both hardened into fact.

Dunmore died in 1809. For lack of a proper biography, we are left with a miniature painted shortly before his death: gray faced and sour, he is the very image of embittered old age.[98] "[I]f the characters of past ages and men are to be drawn at all [wrote Sterne], they are to be drawn like themselves; that is, with their excellences, and with their foibles – and it is as much a piece of justice to the world, to do the one, as the other. –

Lord Dunmore
"The very image of
embittered old age"

The ruling passions . . . are the very things which mark a man's character, in which I would as soon leave out a man's head as his hobbyhorse."[99] To say that Lord Dunmore's primary ruling passion was his own pleasure is merely to state a fact. That does not mean that he was unmanly, lacking in social graces or even for that matter, stupid. His personal library of more than 1,300 volumes was among the largest libraries in North America. If that made Lord Dunmore a pedant he was also "strong built, well shaped with a most frank and open countenance, easy and affable in his manners, very temperate and a great lover of field sports."[100] "[A]s popular as a Scotsman can be amongst weak prejudiced people was how James Parker described him, in a few words linking local disgust over Dunmore's manners with dislike of his ethnic origins.[101] That said, the Shawnee chief who would later wonder out loud to Augustine Prevost, "What old little man is that yonder playing like a boy?" did Dunmore the man a piece of justice. Unfit though he might be in some ways, he was always "jolly, hearty. . . polite & hospitable at his own table."[102]

Other offenses were to follow, not the least of which was Dunmore's reaction to the King's insistence on an annulment of the marriage of his daughter Augusta to the King's son Prince Frederick Augustus on the grounds that they had married without royal permission, as required by the State Marriage Act. Quick as always to defend friends and family, Dunmore demanded an audience with the King, only to be told to his face that the couple's children were "Bastards! Bastards!" Not to be outdone, even by the King, Dunmore replied, "Yes, Sire, just such Bastards as yours are." We are told that the Earl (aged seventy-one) and the King (aged seventy-three) then glared at each other "in apoplectic fury." "God damn him," Dunmore later told his family, "It was as much as I could do to refrain from attempting to knock him down."[103]

A Postscript in the Shandean Manner

What little is known of the later life of Kitty Eustace is sadly not enough to refute F. Scott Fitzgerald's famous observation that there are "no second acts" in American life.[104] Instead of an epilogue, we have a stranger's offhand comment; instead of a letter, an orphan P.S. But while not enough to secure Kitty's place in history, these turn out to just enough to make her unforgettable.

The traveler's sighting of Kitty at a capitol ball in June of 1777 was just four months after she began her new life as the consort of one of the staunchest Whigs in America. It was a remarkably abrupt turnaround for a woman so closely identified with the tyrant Dunmore. "Mrs. Cuthbert (formerly Mrs. Blair, a Daughter of Dr. Eustis of New York)" was how the traveler had described Kitty, and in fact Dixon and Hunter's *Virginia Gazette* for February 14, 1777 duly noted the marriage of "Mrs Catherine Blair of this city [to] Maj. S[eth] J[ohn] Cuthbert of Georgia." It was a society wedding, insofar as that was possible in a time of war, conducted in Bruton Parish Church by Rev John Bracken, with Virginia's first elected governor, Patrick Henry, in attendance.[105] On paper at least, Kitty had traded up: a ranking officer in the Continental Line (and soon-to-be governor of the state of Georgia) for the son of a former acting governor of Virginia — and she was still a "fine dancer."[106]

Exactly how Kitty survived the brutal British occupation of Georgia is less clear. The year 1779 was a a dangerous one for anyone who espoused the rebel cause, let alone the spouse of a rebel. We do know that Kitty and Margaret lived in Savannah until just prior to the British invasion, and that both ladies intended to travel to Philadelphia later in that year to join John Skey Eustace, who was serving as aide de camp (and quondam son)[107] to Maj. Gen. Charles Lee, a turncoat British officer with such a long resume as a warrior that some in Congress wanted him to replace Washington.

Whether mother and daughter actually reached Philadelphia is unknown; only that Kitty, based on the following P.S. to a now lost letter, probably written by her mother, was looking forward to the trip:

Well [she told Lee] I am to Say Something for Myself – then 'over the water, & over the Lee, to Charley' Is the Word – I hope to Be with You Bag & Baggage Before I eat my Christmas Dinner, Mamma Says I must Carry my Cradle, But as I have a Will of my own (& they seem disposed Just Now to Coax Me) I say I won't: You must find the Cage, & I'll bring the Bird, and I will make you a present of them Both As an Addition to your Pets. I am just thinking what Brackenridge will say when we all get together – (We have heard his speech about you already) – Such a family of curiosities as General Lee has got! A Widow that is resolved to live in a State of Monogamy A Settled Serious Politician, as staunch a Whig as ever Shouldered a Musket in America. You shall furnish him with a list of my extraordinary abilities & Genl. Lees adopted Son, a wild, volatile, extravagant fellow, with a little of the Shandean Fun about him; In short a fine Child the Picture of his Pious Daddy – the L[or]d have Mercy upon You! & give you patience & resignation under all those trials. Don't forget to have a Swing ready, I remember a Compliment You Paid me once that you wou'd give a hundred Guineas for my Picture when I was Swinging – If you apply to my Master I dare say you may get the Original for half the Sum – for in real good truth I am a very useless piece of furniture these times. I am not going to Make one word of Apology for all the trouble I am likely to give you – If you wish to lessen it look out for a habitation for us – Neither shall I say a word about the fellow-feeling I have for You, that is an old Story – & I know you hate Repetitions & Parenthesis – And now my Dear Sir believe from the bottom of my soul, & In the sincerity of my heart I wish you & every thing that you like, happiness, and that regard, Esteem& Respect, & every other Word that is made Use of on those occasions Added to Affection, does not express more that I feel for General Lee, as the Guardian & Protector of a beloved & only Brother.

I want to ask you a question – how comes it you never Courted me? I declare I don't think there is any body In the Round World that wou'd have suited you so well. I don't know if I shall forgive you. Your being so partial to Jack has quite mortified Me – And I am sure I am as clever a fellow & have not half his faults. I think the Postscript is long enough, You think so too – So Adieu! Adieu!

C: Cuthbert

August 10th, '79[108]

As is often the case with Kitty, we find we have need of a key to decode her allusions: "Charley over the Water" is an English Nursery Rhyme, made relevant here not only by General Lee's given name, "Charles," but by Charley's love for "a pret–ty girl as sweet as su–gar can–dy." Kitty's reference to "my cradle" tells us that she is a nursing, though not entirely domesticated mother, as she has a will of her own and her mother and husband are unable to coax her to wear her cradle. (During this period, nursing women wore sash-like "cradles" over their shoulders and across their chests, a pleasant arrangement for the baby, but perhaps not for a mother who had hopes of being "courted.") Lee's "pets" refer to a pack of snarling dogs, his usual bed part-ners – along with the odd whore. Brackenridge is Hugh Henry Brackinridge (1748–1816), publisher of the muck-raking news-paper, *United States Magazine*, the first issue of which (published in January of 1779) included a merry, fictitious letter from Gen. Lee to one "Miss Frank." on the subject of the color of his breeches. (Brackenridge's publication of the letter elicited a furious protest and threats of a thrashing from Lee to which Brackenridge responded with frequent public references to Lee as that "ourang outang.") The "Widow" is of course Mar-garet Eustace. Kitty's "Master" is her husband, Seth John Cuth-bert, described here as a "Serious Politician, as staunch a Whig as ever Shouldered a musket." "Jack" is John Skey Eustace; his "Pious Daddy" Dr. Eustace ("pious" is meant to be ironic, an allusion to his passion for the obscene *Tristram Shandy*). The modern equivalent of "family" is "entourage." The term "Guardian & Protector" refers to Gen. Lee's oft-expressed intention to make Jack his son and heir.

Annotation does not do Kitty justice. Her apparently im-promptu P. S. might be the wittiest epistolary performance by a woman to survive from the revolutionary era. At the least, it suggests that Kitty's own sense of Shandean fun included a talent for parody. Not only does her P.S. look like a page out of *Tristram Shandy*, it is Shandean to its very core. "I am sure I am as clever a *fellow* as Jack", says Kitty, in a word twitting the male chauvinist in Lee – even as she points out (quite correctly, as it turns out) that she has not half her brother's faults. She knows that Lee has no good answer to her question, "How comes it you never Courted me?" What matters is that he *should feel that he made a mistake*; that despite being a married woman – and a nursing mother at that – she remains as clever and flirtatious as ever. We are left, finally, as we always are with Kitty, wanting to know more than the historical record can say.[109]

Our problem is further aggravated by the aura of mystery surrounding her marriage. In a letter written six months after Kitty's P.S., her brother reminded Gen. Lee of his promise to write "Major Cuthbert, as the happiness of our family rests solely (almost) on your decision."[110] Was Kitty's allusion to being "a very useless piece of furniture" to her husband more than hyperbole? Was her marriage on the rocks? Did she mean her question to be taken seriously, as an invitation? Unfortunately, we will probably never know, as any further communication between Gen. Lee and his adoptive family of curiosities, was terminated just four months later by John Skey Eustace. "I am perfectly tired of having my peace of mind disturbed by the daily alterations in your temper," Jack wrote to Lee, proving that his sister's description of him as a wild, volatile fellow was no exaggeration.[111]

The remaining known facts of Kitty's life indicate a decidedly downward trajectory. We know that Seth John Cuthbert remarried in 1785; that his second wife, herself the daughter of a former governor, was Mary Clay; that she bore him two sons, and that Cuthbert died in 1788. We can surmise from Kitty's reference to a cradle in her 1779 P.S. that she had just had a baby. But we know nothing about her child's fate, how long she lived with Cuthbert or when she died.[112] From a November 13, 1788 notice in the *Georgia Gazette*, we know that Mrs. Margaret Eustace applied for letters of administration for the estate of "Catherine Cuthbert (formerly Catherine Blair)" That does not mean however that Kitty died in 1788 or that Mary Clay's husband was a bigamist. Certainly there is no record of a divorce, though Cuthbert, as a former governor of Georgia and as a prominent, current member of the Georgia Assembly, could have had one for the asking.[113] We may not have all the facts. But we do have Kitty's literary remains: her P.S. and her letters. Unlike in style though they may be, they are equally radical in the claims they make on her male readers. Kitty not only sees herself as the intellectual equal of any man; she sees herself as just as *powerful*. She is in that respect a modern woman, so prodigal of her charms, mental and physical, that she can call herself "a useless piece of baggage" (to Lee) and tell Burke she is "grown prodigiously fat."[114] In short, it is simply impossible to imagine Kitty Eustace enacting the most rigid duties of a good wife.

Jack Eustace's later life turned out to be a vindication of his sister's better judgment. It would take too long to recount all of his exploits but a few will suffice to show his character. Having begun the war by betraying his patron, Jack might have hesitated before betraying the land of his fathers. But it seems that he did not. Within days, he had found his way onto the staff of Charles Lee. A six-year stint in the Continental Army was to follow, during which 16-year-old *Major* Jack Eustace was concurrently cited for bravery and suspected of disloyalty following Lee's 1777 court martial – only to find redemption as a valued aide de camp to both Gen. John Sullivan and Gen. Nathaniel Greene.

Jack resigned from the American army in 1780, though it seems not from the war, as he continued to serve in the Georgia Militia. In 1782 he secured a law license and for a year served as Adjutant General of the State of Georgia. In 1784 he went to South America, intending to lend a hand in the fight against Spanish tyranny. In 1792, he joined the French army; and for a while acted as aide de camp to Francisco de Miranda, an aptly-named "soldier of misfortune" whose particular obsession was the liberation of Venezuela, but who was then fighting in the French revolutionary army against the Prussians and Austrians. In 1793, Jack turned against Miranda, assailing him in a pamphlet that was so bitter and so detailed that it was used as a bill of particulars in Miranda's later prosecution for desertion. There would be other fallings in and fallings out in Spain and Holland; but apparently not in France, where *Major General* Eustace was last seen commanding a French division in Flanders. A Congressional ban against Americans serving in foreign armies sent Eustace scurrying home – after a stop in London where he was jailed for publishing a pamphlet on "the crimes of George III." We know what happened next, because like everything else in his life, he wrote a book about it. It was called "Exile of Major General Eustace, a Citizen of the United States of America from . . . Great Britain, by order of His Grace the Duke of Portland, Minister for the Home Department."[115] On his return to New York in 1798, he joined his mother at "Campbell Hall," the Orange County cottage built by his grandfather Laughlin Campbell. He was as close to being home as he would ever be.

Jack died in 1805; only to live again in a fervent, deathbed hosanna to his Christian faith – this after spending most of his life consorting with malcontents, deists and apostates – dictated to a friend who arranged for its publication in the *New York Gazette*. He remains one of the most intriguing figures to emerge from the Revolution, a worthy subject, as one historian has recently suggested, for a biographical study of his own.[116]

His mother, whose demise was fleetingly noted in a Newburgh newspaper, died four years later. Though she appears on the New York tax list for 1772 as a land owner, her holdings fall far short of "the vast territorial property" her son had once called "the patrimony of my noble ancestors."[117] Our last glimpse of Margaret and Jack comes from a 1846 history of Orange County, New York. Though it errs in describing Margaret as having lived for many years in the south with her husband, it captures the air of injured dignity, unrequited neediness and greed that was both her assumed character and her fate:

> When the writer was a small lad, Mrs. Eustace resided at Campbell Hall [her father's farm in Orange County.] For dignity of manner, good sense and lady-like deportment she had few equals at the time in that part of the country. Doct. Eustace, her husband, was from the South, and she resided there with him for many years There was a family secret, which we never fully understood, and which deeply embittered the last years of the life of Mrs. Eustace and that of her son the General. *De Mortuis nil nisi bonum.* ["Speak nothing but good of the dead."][118]

What dark secret harried Margaret and Maj. Gen. John Skey Eustace to their graves? Was it Kitty's affair with Lord Dunmore, who lived to be despised on both sides of the Atlantic? Was it Kitty's failed first marriage, the loss of her child or some tragic aspect of her own death? Was it John Skey Eustace making himself *persona non grata* in virtually every nation in Europe? Was it the loss, after so many years and petitions, of the noble patrimony of Laughlin Campbell? Was it, simply (to paraphrase Sterne), the family propensity for seizing the wrong end of the stick?

We may never know. Meanwhile, scholarly research into this most intriguing of American families continues.

The remains of Dunmore's palace

A World Big with Jest

In *Tristram Shandy*, Sterne wrote, "Everything in the world . . . is big with jest – and has wit in it, and instruction in it too – if we can but find it out?"[119] So where is the jest, let alone the wit and instruction, in this ribald tale of a royal governor and his not-so-coy mistress? For Virginia's Whigs, the joke was clearly on Lord Dunmore, whose conduct spawned a revolution. For his Lordship, it was always on the Virginians, whom he damned as authors of their own misery. That left the score Virginia one, Dunmore one. But what about Kitty and her family of curiosities? They had known injustice, scandal and, if we include Dr. Eustace's flight to Wilmington, desertion. Where was the jest in that? What can a bold, witty young woman of 19 tell us about the spirit of the age?

At the conclusion of *Tristram Shandy*, Sterne quotes Tristram's mother as asking: "L[or]d . . . what is all this story about?" It seems a rather good question to ask at the end of a novel which makes so many demands on the reader without gratifying his need for an explanation. "A COCK and a BULL . . . And one of the best of its kind, I ever heard"[120] says Yorick/Sterne – all of which has elicited a fair amount of speculation about Sterne's authorial aims and intentions. Clearly America's Founders were not in doubt. *Tristram Shandy* was one of their favorite books.[121] John Adams thought it "droll and funny," while Thomas and Martha Jefferson drew their final adieu from it.[122]

We could say simply that *Tristram Shandy* is a strange book and leave it at that.[123] But how do we explain its appeal to a readership that included both a Dunmore and a Jefferson? And what was it about Sterne's great work that spoke to the radical sensibility of a Kitty Eustace? The answer lies in the recognition that *Tristram Shandy* is not a novel but the parody of a novel; not so much a satire of Eighteenth Century sentimental excess as an authentic expression of it. The Kitty Eustace of her letter to Ann Blair is not simply bold; she is empowered. Similarly, though her P.S. to Lee and her letter to Thomas Burke can be read as merely coquettish, they can also be read as *parodies of that style*, an easy task for someone whose taste in novels ran the gamut from *Tristram Shandy* to anonymous bodice rippers like *Cleora or the Fair Inconstant*. When twenty-two-year-old Kitty tells poet, doctor-lawyer, soon-to-be governor Thomas Burke, that she knows something of the theory of things, she is speaking to him *as a man*, not a woman. Pretty she may be; clever for sure. But her manner of speaking is also a deliberate assault on male hegemony, the more seductive for being sourced in an iron-clad conviction that she is a damn fine woman.

The best books of an era are not always our best guides to the character of the era. That would seem especially true when the era in question is a time of revolutionary upheaval. If so, *Tristram Shandy* (an odd man out if there ever was one) is an exception that proves the rule. Instead of a logical, well-crafted story set in a familiar landscape populated by life-like characters, we are given a plot-less, intentionally illogical succession of scenes accented by histrionic voices – from Tristram's on again, off again narrative of his creation (told from the sperm's point of view) to Uncle Toby's refrain that Dr. Slop had never "seen the prodigious armies we had in Flanders."[124] Sterne is not an easy read. But that is not because his diction is difficult; it is because his subject is revolution.

We can see how the Eustaces (like Jane Austen's Bennetts)

might have provided "sport for [their] neighbors."[125] The gold
digger (Kitty) who refuses to be tempted by guilt; the wild,
romantic boy (Jack) who drifts from revolution to revolution in
search of something or someone, perhaps a father; the matri-
arch (Margaret) who espouses monogamy for honorable
mention as the best of mothers – the father (Dr. Eustace) who
trades the duties of a father for the frisks and curvets of a novelist: the Eustaces belie virtually everything we were taught to
believe about the so called Age of Reason. In fact, it was not
logical, not stoical, and the dour face of George Washington on
the one dollar bill – a face that for many still defines the era –
is as unlike the age as it is the character of Washington himself.

To borrow another phrase from Charles Dickens, the Age of
Revolution was the "best of times . . . the worst of times; "the
age of foolishness . . . the epoch of incredulity."[126] It was also
the age of injustice, outrage and hyperbole; a time for satire,
lies and damn lies. The Whig caricature of Dunmore as the
person best fitted to ruin Britain's cause and procure union and
success for America is only slightly more valid than other cari-
catures of the period. What made the charge stick was his
Lordship's inability to sustain the character he was assigned.
He was not courtly and dignified like Botetourt. He was dis-
armingly friendly, devious and crude. Before there was
Dunmore the boor, there was American fascination with the
British aristocracy. Before there were Stamp Act riots, there
was British preoccupation with American ingratitude. Still to
be accounted for is revolution on a personal level, the kind of
revolution embodied in Kitty Eustace's refusal to admit guilt
and in her bold question, "How comes it you never Courted
me?" In an era in which George Washington struggled con-
stantly to stay in character, Kitty was always herself.

Those who wish to know the causes that "impelled [Amer-
ica] to the separation" should read Thomas Jefferson's powerful

(and highly seductive) Declaration of Independence. Those who wish to experience the *feeling* of revolution should look at a page from *Tristram Shandy*. No one captures the true, rebellious spirit of the Eighteenth Century better than Lawrence Sterne. But if you want to know why Americans equated liberty with emotional release, read Kitty's P.S. A woman much ahead of her time, Kitty shows us how a true feeler enacts liberty in her own life; not with fiery manifestoes but with radical arrogations of power in an environment of constraint.

Sent along with Dr. Eustace's letter to Sterne was a piece of what the doctor called "Shandean statuary" – a "singular" walking stick previously owned by the late Gov. Arthur Dobbs of North Carolina. It was a gift, Eustace said, offered in the hope that Sterne might find it an apt subject for meditation. In his reply, Sterne thanked Eustace for the gift but disagreed it was a parallel for *Tristram Shandy:* "The parallel breaks . . . in this, that, in using the stick everyone will take the handle which suits his convenience. In *Tristram Shandy*, the handle is taken which suits their passions, their ignorance or sensibility."[127] Dunmore did not ruin Britain's cause. It was ruined by irrepressible men and women seizing the handle best suited to their sensibility; that is, the handle of themselves as genuine American originals.

Notes

1 Quoted in Frank L. Dewey,. "Thomas Jefferson and a Williamsburg Scandal: The Case of *Blair v. Blair*," *Virginia Magazine of History and Biography* (1981) 89: 49–50. But for Frank Dewey the entertaining and (I would argue) important story of Kitty Eustace and Lord Dunmore might have been lost to history. I am deeply indebted to him.

2 Wills Hill, 1st Marquess of Downshire, known as Viscount Hillsborough from 1742 to 1751 and the Earl of Hillsborough from 1751 to 1789, Secretary of State for the Colonies from 1768 to 1772. George III once described Lord Hillsborough as "amiable" but "the least man of business I ever knew" – competent enough when the issues were straightforward but a total ass where anything complicated was concerned. King George III to Lord North, 27 Mar. 1782, in Sir John Fortescue, ed., *The Correspondence of King George the Third from 1760 to December 1783*, (6 vols.; London 1927–28), 5: 418.

3 The King's draftsmen completed work on Dunmore's Commission on December 6. The privy seal was affixed on January 2, 1771. Addressed in the King's Instructions as "my Right trusty and Right well-beloved cousin," Lord Dunmore's formal title was "Earl of Dunmore, Viscount Fincastle, and Baron of Blair, Mouilli and Fillimet."

4 "Lords Debate," 2 Jan.1770, *Proceedings and Debates of the British Parliament Respecting North America, 1754–1783*, R.C. Simmons and P.D.G. Thomas, eds. (5 vols.; New York, 1984) 3: 165–166.

5 *Virginia Gazette*, (Dixon & Hunter) 5 Aug. 1775

6 See Earl of Hillsborough to Lord Dunmore, 11 Feb. 1771 quoted in Percy Burdelle Caley, *Dunmore: Colonial Governor of New York and Virginia, 1770 – 1782*, (Ph.d diss.; Pittsburgh, 1939), p. 84 (citing "Public Record Office, C.O. 5, 1349, p. 83, Library of Congress Transcripts.") Lord Dunmore's Instructions were enclosed with Hillsborough's letter of February 11. According to Caley, Dunmore received his instructions by "the last of March." Caley, *Dunmore: Colonial Governor of New York and Virginia*, p. 84.

If so, he was at least two weeks behind the Virginians, who read about his appointment in Purdie and Dixon's March 7, 1771 *Virginia Gazette*.

7 Earl of Dunmore to Earl of Hillsborough, 2 July 1771, K. G. Davies, ed., *Documents of the American Revolution, 1770–1783*, (21 vols.; New York, 1984) 3: 127–126.

8 The directive that Dunmore "lose no time in repairing" to Virginia can be found in Hillsborough's February 11 letter. Caley, *Dunmore: Colonial Governor of New York and Virginia*, p. 84. Dunmore's Instructions drove the point home, ordering him "to fit yourself with all convenient speed, and . . . repair to our said Colony of Virginia." *Ibid.*

9 Earl of Dunmore to Earl of Hillsborough, 2 July 1771, Davies, ed., *Documents of the American Revolution, 1770–1783*, 3: 127–126.

10 The lost private letter to Lord Hillsborough was dated 9 Mar. 1771. See Earl of Dunmore to Earl of Hillsborough, 4 June 1771, Davies, ed., *Documents of the American Revolution, 1770–1783*, 3: 107.

11 *Ibid.*

12 For the details of Dunmore's great New York land grab see Caley, *Dunmore: Colonial Governor of New York and Virginia*, pp. 19–37.

13 See Caley, *Dunmore: Colonial Governor of New York and Virginia, 1770 – 1782*, p. 81 and p. 82, n. 12.

14 Earl of Dunmore to Earl of Hillsborough, 4 June 1771, Davies, ed., *Documents of the American Revolution,1770–1783*, 3:107.

15 William Smith, *Historical Memoirs from 16 March to 25 July 1778*, William H. W. Sabine, ed. (2 vols.; New York, 1958), 1:105.

16 William Tryon to Earl of Hillsborough, 31 Aug. 1771, Colonial Office Papers, Public Record Office, 5:154 (Private Miscellaneous Correspondence.)

17 *Ibid.*

18 Smith, *Historical Memoirs*, 1:105, 107. Dunmore may have *seen* Flanders while he was serving in the 3rd Regiment of Foot Guards (1749 to 1758), but that is about all. By the time he enlisted in the Guards, elements of which were present at two Flanders battlefields – Fontenoy (1745) and Lauffield (1747) – the War of Austrian Succession was already over. Whether or not his reference to Tryon's "never seeing Flanders" was meant to echo the opening lines of Lawrence Sterne's popular novel, *The Life and Opinions of Tristram Shandy*, is an interesting, if entirely unanswerable question. "I wish, Dr. Slop," Uncle Toby says on the novel's opening page, "you had seen what prodigious armies we had in Flanders."

19 Benson J. Lossing, ed., "Grants of Land in Vermont," *The American Historical Record*, II (March, 1873), p.100ff; Horatio Rogers, ed., *Hadden's Journal and Orderly Books* (Albany, 1884), App. 5, p. 381f. For a more scholarly discussion of this transaction see, Caley, "Dunmore: Colonial Governor of New York and Virginia: 1770 – 1781,"pp. 19–37.

20 Richard Bland to Thomas Adams, 1 Aug. 1771 in *William and Mary Quarterly*, (Jan., 1897), 5: 156.

21 *Ibid.*

22 Mary Horsmanden, the daughter of Virginia immigrants Daniel Horsmanden and Ursula St. Leger, married William Byrd III's grandfather, Williams Byrd 1, in 1673. It was her second marriage.

23 William Nelson to the Earl of Hillsborough, 1 July 1771, in John C. Van Horne, ed., *The Correspondence of William Nelson as Acting Governor of Virginia, 1770–1771*, (Charlottesville, 1975) pp. 151–152. Nelson was apparently too discreet to mention that Dunmore had told him that "he like[d] . . . New York so well" that he was seeking "leave to remain." That Nelson might take offence at his "continuing . . . desir[e]" for New York over Virginia never even entered Dunmore's mind. See Caley, *Dunmore: Colonial Governor of New York and Virginia: 1770 – 1781*, p. 81.

24 *Virginia Gazette* (Purdie and Dixon), 11 July 1771.

25 *Virginia Gazette* (Purdie and Dixon), 18 July 1771.

26 *Ibid.*

27 For his ride from Yorktown to Williamsburg, Dunmore was accompanied by Council members William Nelson, John Page and Robert Carter III. See *Virginia Gazette* (Purdie and Dixon), 26 Sept. 1771. The description of Kitty as "pretty" is from a letter of Mrs. James Parker, describing the summertime plans of "Mrs. Eustace and her pretty daughter," "[T]hey are really two very agreeable ladies," Mrs. Parker added. Mrs. James Parker to Charles Steuart, 15 Aug. 1770, *Charles Steuart Papers*, National Library of Scotland, Edinburgh, MS 5040, ff. 76–77, by gracious permission of the Trustees of the National Library of Scotland.

28 *Virginia Gazette* (Rind); 26 Sep. 1771; *Virginia Gazette* (Purdie and Dixon) 26 Sep. 1771. To be fully appreciated, the perfunctory welcome accorded Dunmore must be laid alongside Acting Governor William Nelson's eulogy to Botetourt on the occasion of the July 11, 1771 reopening of the Assembly. See "Address of the President of the Council to the Council and House of Burgesses," condoling with them on the loss of Botetourt and hoping his successor "would be equally entitled to [their] . . . esteem." in

Virginia Gazette (Purdie and Dixon) 11 July 1771.

29 Edmund Randolph, *History of Virginia*, ed., Arthur H. Shaffer (Charlottesville, 1970), p. 197. Despite what is commonly believed, drunkenness was not one of Dunmore's depravities. Indeed, if the "hundreds of bottles of sherry wine" noted in a 1775 Palace inventory are proof of anything, it is that the Governor loved a social glass. (It would have been more scandalous for the host of first resort in Virginia *not* to pass the bottle).

30 *Letters of Richard Henry Lee*, James Curtis Ballagh, ed., (2 vols.; Charlottesville, 1911–1914) 1:162.

31 James Parker to Charles Steuart, 18 Nov. 1772, *Charles Steuart Papers*, MS 5027, ff. 249–50.

32 Dr. Eustace's first documented appearance in Wilmington was in connection with the trial of Alexander Simpson, Master of the sloop *Viper*, following his fatal duel with Lt. Whitehurst, also of the *Viper*. The duel occurred on 18 March 1764. See letter and "related documents" from Lt. Gov. William Tryon to the Board of Trade of Great Britain, June 24, 1765, http://docsouth.unc.edu/csr/index.html/document/csr07-0024 (accessed 12 December 2009.)

33 In his account of the scandal, Frank L Dewey notes that Margaret's brother Donald Campbell "claimed" kinship with the Duke of Argyll and the Earl of Loudon. As if by contrast (and without attribution), Dewey describes Dunmore as "a kinsman of unspecified degree." What this all amounts to is hard to say, as extensive research has so far failed to yield any basis for a claim of kinship, let alone specify its degree. See Frank L. Dewey, *Thomas Jefferson Lawyer*, p. 58

34 John Hill Wheeler, *Historical Sketches of North Carolina from 1584 to 1851* (Philadelphia: Clearfield Co., 1851; Baltimore: Regional Publishing Co., 1964), pp. 284–285. Citations are to the Regional Pub. Co. edition.

35 *Ibid*; George Birkbeck Hill ed., *Boswell's Life of Johnson*, (6 vols.; London, 1934) 2: 222, n. 2. "'I was but once,' Johnson said, "in Sterne's company, and then his only attempt at merriment consisted in his display of a drawing too indecently gross to have delighted even in a brothel."

36 Wheeler, *Historical Sketches of North Carolina*, pp. 284–285.

37 Dr. Campbell's kinship relationship with the Eustaces is unclear.

38 According to James Parker, his first encounter with Margaret and Kitty Eustace occurred shortly before the 10th of November, 1769 "I received your letter by Mrs. Eustace [Parker wrote Charles Steuart] and have waited on her. She is a very agreeable chearfull woman & her daughter a

pretty, smart girl." James Parker to Charles Steuart, 10 Nov. 1769, *Charles Steuart Papers*, MS 5040, ff. 76–77.

39 James Parker to Charles Steuart, 3 May 1771, *Charles Steuart Papers*, MS 5020, f. 265.

40 See "Deposition of John Blair in the Lawsuit of *Margaret Eustace v. Seth John Cuthbert*," (1786) *Blair Family Papers, 1741–1792.* Special Collections Research Center, Swem Library, College of William and Mary.

41 The former governors were Francis Fauquier 1758–1768) and Robert Dinwiddie (1751–1758). John Blair died on November 5, 1771, less than six months after his son's marriage to Kitty, John Blair Sr., died. He was thus providentially spared a scandal that may well have killed him – as it probably did his son.

42 Arthur Lee to John Blair Sr., January 1, 1770; Arthur Lee to James Blair, [1770], quoted in Dewey, *Thomas Jefferson, Lawyer*, p. 58.

43 The explanation of John Randolph, given in county court, was that James "left the house in which they were" (i.e., the Blair house in Williamsburg) and that Kitty, finding herself "deserted . . . then removed to [her mother's lodging house for William and Mary students] not 100 paces off." For the full argument of John Randolph in *Blair v. Blair*, see Dewey, "Thomas Jefferson and a Williamsburg Scandal: The Case of *Blair v. Blair*," *Virginia Magazine of History and Biography* (1981) 89: 49–57, 50.

44 Based on surviving records, Margaret Eustace appeared as a trustee or plaintiff in at least four lawsuits, including (besides Kitty's suit against Dr. Blair), a joint action with her siblings to enforce the promise of Gov. W.E. Cosby of New York, a collection action against a debtor to the estate of Dr. John Eustace and a lawsuit brought after Kitty's death against Seth John Cuthbert, for the recovery of her dowry.

45 Kitty Eustace Blair to Ann Blair, 18 July 1772, *Tucker-Coleman Papers.* 1664–1945. Special Collections Research Center, Swem Library, College of William and Mary.

46 Frank L. Dewey, "Thomas Jefferson's Notes on Divorce," *The William and Mary Quarterly*, Third Series, (Jan. 1982), 39: 212–223. To be precise, these were notes *for* a brief, not the thing itself. Still, it is hard to see how Pendleton, Mercer and Jefferson could have avoided running wild in the field of law, given the lack of legal precedent for their position.

47 James Parker to Charles Steuart, 25 May 1771, *Charles Steuart Papers*, MS 5027, ff. 159–60.

48 *Ibid.*

49 James Blair to St. George Tucker, 15 Sept. 1772, in the *Tucker-Coleman Papers*.

50 Margaret Eustace to Thomas Burke, 4 Nov. 1773, in the *Thomas Burke Papers*, #104, Southern Historical Collection, The Wilson Library, University of North Carolina at Chapel Hill.

51 According to both Parker and John Randolph, the James City County Clerk of Court referred Kitty's case to "arbitration." Classically defined, arbitration requires an arbitrator and an enforceable agreement by the parties to be bound by the arbitrator's decision. For one reason or another, that did not happen in this case, probably because the parties were unwilling to be bound. With that in mind, I believe the most appropriate modern term for what happened in this case (that is, a year-long, court-supervised effort to reach a negotiated settlement) is "mediation." See John Randolph's arguments in *Blair v. Blair* in Dewey, "Thomas Jefferson and a Williamsburg Scandal: The Case of *Blair v. Blair*," VMHB (1981) 89: 50, 55; James Parker to Charles Steuart, 12 Jun, 1772, *Charles Steuart Papers*, MS 5027, f. 178.

52 James Parker to Charles Steuart, 25 May 1772, *Charles Steuart Papers*, MS 5027, ff. 159–60.

53 James Parker to Charles Steuart, 12 Jun 1772, *Charles Steuart Papers*, MS 5027, f. 178

54 Frank Dewey, relying on Kitty's statement that the letter fell into her hands "the Evening after," assumed that she meant *after* the Dunmore-brokered reconciliation, but *before* James's push. If that is so, it would help to explain why Kitty, anticipating failure (or worse), should have immediately "jumped out of bed." Frank L. Dewey, *Thomas Jefferson, Lawyer* (Charlottesville, Va., 1986), p. 60. See James Parker to Charles Steuart, 12 Jun. 1772, *Charles Steuart Papers*, MS 5027, f. 178.

55 Quoted in Dewey, *Thomas Jefferson, Lawyer*, p. 60.

56 Kitty Eustace Blair to Ann Blair, 18 July 1772, *Tucker-Coleman Papers*. At the time she wrote this letter, Kitty was nineteen years old.

57 *Ibid.*

58 *Ibid.*

59 One of Parker's terms for the Virginia aristocracy. See also James Parker to Charles Steuart, 20 Feb. 1773, *Charles Steuart Papers*, MS 5028, ff. 32–33.

60 Josiah Quincy, "A Journal, 1773," in Jane Carson, ed., *We Were There: Descriptions of Williamsburg, 1699–1859* (Williamsburg, 1965), p. 28.

61 "I should not need to mention the unutterable horrors that took possession

of my bosom, when I perused this *accursed letter*, by which I learned the apostacy, disobedience, and degeneracy of my idolized Serafina" (italics supplied.), Tobias Smollett, *The Adventures of Peregrine Pickle*, in *Works of Tobias Smollett* (Mobile Reference; Kindle Edition, 2003–2005), loc. 2226; "[H]e had it now in his power to retort the contempt of the world in a manner suited to his *most sanguine wish*," *ibid.*, loc. 18797 (italics supplied). Kitty's term for her mother, "the best of parents," comes from Henry Fielding's *History of Tom Jones, A Foundling* (Distributive Proofreaders, Kindle Edition, no date), loc. 2617: "He well knew that fortune is generally the principal, if not the sole, consideration, which operates on *the best of parents* in these matters" (italics supplied.) The passage describes the scheming of Tom Jones, a bastard, to secure the hand of Squire Western's daughter, a gloss, in some ways, on the efforts of the clever, managing Margaret Eustace, to marry Kitty into the Blair family. For a complete list of the 262 volumes in Kitty's library, see "An Inventory of the Personal Estate of Dr. John Eustace, Deceased," by J. Bryan Grimes, Secretary of State, *North Carolina Wills and Inventories*, (Baltimore, 1967), pp. 490–494.

[62] Under the law of coverture, ownership of a woman's property passed to her husband at the time of marriage.

[63] Margaret Eustace to James Blair and James Blair to St. George Tucker, both dated 15 Sept. 1772, *Tucker-Coleman Papers*.

[64] Quoted in John E. Selby, *Dunmore* (Virginia Bicentennial Commission, Williamsburg, Va., 1977), p. 13.

[65] M. D. Conway, *Omitted Chapters of History Disclosed in the Life and Papers of Edmund Randolph*, (New York, 1889), p. 14.

[66] James Parker to Charles Steuart, 18 Nov. 1772, Charles Steuart Papers, quoted in Frank L. Dewey, "Thomas Jefferson and a Williamsburg Scandal: *The Case of Blair v. Blair*," pp. 45–46. In alluding to "the goodness of the blood," Parker was apparently raising the question as to whether Dr. Blair's sexual incompetence might have a genetic cause, or in 18th century parlance, be due to "a weakness of the blood."

[67] James Parker to Charles Steuart, 20 Feb. 1773, *Charles Steuart Papers*, MS 5028, f. 32.

[68] James Parker to Charles Steuart, 19 May 1773, *Charles Steuart Papers*, MS 5028, f. 373.

[69] "Sukey" is a common Eighteenth-Century nickname for Susanna. "Diary of Augustine Prevost," in Wainwright, "Turmoil at Pittsburgh: Diary of Augustine Prevost, 1774," p. 124.

70 Parker's code word for sex is "paa." Lord knows why.

71 James Parker to Charles Steuart, May 19, 1773, *Charles Steuart Papers*, MS 5028, ff. 373.

72 That is, sometime *after* James Parker's letter of May 19, 1773 and *before* the General Court rendered judgment on November 3, 1773. The "professed slave of Miss Blair" has not been identified.

73 James Parker to Charles Steuart, 14 Nov. 1773, *Charles Steuart Papers*, ms 5028, f.139. So far, research has failed to identify the "Mrs. Blair" who testified for the defense. Parker called her "a Hardiman" (a well known Virginia family) and the "widow of Chowder" (a name which rings no bells.) She could not be the wife of John Blair Sr., as her maiden name was Mary Monro. Nor could she be Jean Blair, maiden name Blair, the wife of John Blair Jr. and (according to him) Kitty Eustace's good friend.

74 Margaret Eustace to Thomas Burke, 4 Nov. 1773, *Thomas Burke Papers*. Joy, relief and the fact that she was writing to a poet only go so far in explaining Margaret's love of hyperbole. In fact, curvets and frisks of sentiment were a family trait.

75 *Ibid.*

76 Lawrence Sterne to Dr. John Eustace, February 9, 1768, Lydia Sterne de Medalle ed., *The Works of Lawrence Sterne*, (8 vols.; London 1790) 6: 250–253.

77 Interestingly, Randolph made no attempt to defend Kitty's claim (in a pretrial deposition) that she was still a virgin, noting if she was a "vestal . . . she mean[t it] in mente tantum, as Lucretia did. '*Corpus est tantum violatum, animus insons.*'"

78 See "An Argument before the General Court of Colonial Virginia, Anne Blair widow of Dr. Blair his Executor, Nov. 1773" in Dewey, "Thomas Jefferson and a Williamsburg Scandal: *The Case of Blair v. Blair*," *pp. 52, 49–57* (Jefferson's caption is confusing. It should read something like this, "Catherine Blair, Widow of Dr. Blair v. Ann Blair, Executrix of the Estate of Dr. Blair." Dewey.)

79 *Ibid.*

80 See argument of Edmund Pendleton in Dewey, "Thomas Jefferson and a Williamsburg Scandal, The Case of *Blair v. Blair*," pp. 59–63,

81 Dunmore's long campaign to deprive Lt. Gov. Colden of his rightful share of the governor's salary is fully documented in Caley, *Dunmore: Colonial Governor of New York and Virginia*, pp. 56–77. As Caley notes, Dunmore was not without legal justification for his lawsuit. The problem, as always with

Dunmore, was how he went about it. See Caley, p. 57.

82   *Virginia Gazette*, (Purdie and Dixon), 20 Dec. 1773.

83   Kitty's lawyer in James City County Court, James Hubbard, was a well-regarded practitioner "in and about Williamsburg," with practice spcialties in admiralty and real estate. See *Virginia Gazette (*Purdie and Dixon), 12 Sep. 1777.

84   Catherine Blair to Thomas Burke, 18 Nov. 1774, *Thomas Burke Papers.*

85   John Blair to Mary Braxton, 13 Mar. 1777, *Blair Family Papers.*

86   "[June] 5th [1777] The Entertainment last Night was very fine, the Music excellent, the Assembly large & polite & the Ladies made a brilliant Appearance . . . . After the Entertainment was over, the Company went up stairs to dance. I think a Mrs. Cuthbert, formerly Mrs. Blair, a Daughter of Dr. Eustis [sic] of New York, made the best Appearance as a dancer," Ebenezer Hazard, "MS Journal of Journeys to the South," 1777–78, 2 vols., Virginia Portion, 1777: May 22–July 3, Nov. 11–Dec. 17). Hist. Soc. Of Penna., MS No. 1398 (reprinted in *We Were There*, p. 38.)

87   The ship was the *H.M.S. Fowey*. One reason that Dunmore may have chosen to remove himself from the city, was the recent discovery that he had buried several barrels of gunpowder in the yard of the powder magazine, thereby giving rise to rumors that he intended to blow up Williamsburg. See *Virginia Gazette* (Pinkney), 8 Jun. 1775.

88   For brief descriptions of the sorts of claims taken under review by the Royal Commission, See, *The Royal Commission of the Losses and Services of American Loyalists 1783–1785*, ed. Hugh Edgar Edgerton (reprint; New York, 1971).

89   "Your Lordship must be thoroughly sensible how pleasing it is to the people to observe, that immediate attention is paid to their affairs, and quick dispatch given thereto." Letter from Lord Dunmore to Lord Hillsborough, [May? 1771] as quoted in Caley, *Dunmore: Colonial Governor of New York and Virginia*, p. 53.

90   Quoted in Caley, *Dunmore: Colonial Governor of New York and Virginia*, p. 332. Caley's source was Virgil Lewis, a descendant of Col. Andrew Lewis, the commander of the Virginia militia in Dunmore's War. Another commentator, also quoted by Caley, found Dunmore "deserve[d] unlimited praise for his great personal sacrifices in defense of the people under his government." *Ibid.*

91   Randolph, *History of Virginia*, p. 91.

92   James Parker to Charles Steuart, 19 May 1773, *Charles Steuart Papers*, MS

5028, ff. 73–71. John Randolph, along with his wife and children (Edmund excepted) set sail for England on September 7, 1775. Speaking of John Randolph's personal character, John Page later recalled, "I faithfully supported the rights and privileges of both Professors and Students [at William and Mary]; and notwithstanding I had been placed [on] . . . the Council . . . by Lord Dunmore, I opposed his nomination of John Randolph as a [Member of the William and Mary Board of Visitors], boldly declaring that as he had been rejected on a former occasion, as not possessing the disposition and character, moral and religious, which the Charter and Statutes of the College required, he ought not again to be nominated, till it could be proved that he had abandoned his former principles, and practices, which no one could venture to say he had." Quoted in Jane Carson, *James Innes and His Brothers of the F.H.C.*, (Colonial Williamsburg Foundation, Williamsburg, VA, 1965), p. 80.

93 The charge that Dunmore "burned" Norfolk can be found in paragraph 26 of the Declaration of Independence: "He [the King] has . . . burned our towns." While the word "candid" (in paragraph 2) does not have quite the same meaning in Jefferson's day as it does today – that is, frank – it has always imported fairness. And to be perfectly fair, Jefferson was choosing to overlook persistent rumors that Norfolk was put to the torch by Virginia and North Carolina troops under the command of Cols. Robert Howe and William Woodford – rumors that within the year would be found to be fact by the Virginia Assembly. The suggestion that Virginians should be made to suffer is contained in a December 24, 1774 letter to Lord Hillsborough: "These undutiful people should be made to feel the distress and misery of which they have themselves laid the foundation." Lord Dunmore to Lord Hillsborough, 24 Dec. 1774, *Documents of the American Revolution*, 8: 267.

94 Nicholas B. Wainwright "Turmoil at Pittsburgh: Diary of Augustine Prevost, 1774, *The Pennsylvania Magazine of History and Biography*, (April 1961) 85: 111–162, 123.

95 "Free Thoughts on the Present Times and Measures," by a Virginian, *Virginia Gazette*, (Pinkney), 29 June 1775.

96 Jack told Gen. Washington that his traveling companion, a British officer, was concealing Lord Dunmore's military plans in the pommel of his saddle. See George Washington to John Hancock, 19 Dec. 1775, *The Papers of George Washington, Revolutionary War Series* ed. W.W. Abbott, et al., (University of Virginia, Charlottesville, Va, 1987), 2:581–582. In his letter to Gen. William Howe, Dunmore described John Skey Eustace as the

"Son of an unfortunate widow Gentlewoman in this Country [Virginia], I have had the Care of Him for these three Years past, and have given him the best Education this Country could afford."

97 Wainwright, ed., "Turmoil at Pittsburgh: Diary of Augustine Prevost, 1774," pp. 123, 143. Prevost did not identify the young lady or his source. But it seems safe to assume that the rumors noted by Jefferson in November of 1773 and the "scandalous chronicle" noted by Prevost nine months later concerned the same two subjects: that is, Lord Dunmore and Kitty.

98 Following a return engagement in the House of Lords (1780–1788), Dunmore was appointed governor of the Bahamas. Once again, he showed abysmally bad judgment, this time by insisting on the construction, at tax-payer expense, of a vast fortification to be named (naturally) "Fort Dunmore." This time, London could not wait to fire him; the proof of his ineptitude was too clear.

99 Lawrence Sterne to Dr. John Eustace, 9 Feb. 1768, *The Works of Lawrence Sterne*, 6: 250–253.

100 James Rivington to Sir William Johnson, 22 Oct. 1770, in Alexander C. Flick, ed., *The Papers of Sir William Johnson*, (14 vols.; Albany, University of the State of New York, 1921—1965), 7:945. It was Edmund Randolph who described Dunmore as a "pedant." See Randolph, *History of Virginia*, p.196

101 Quoted in John E. Selby, *Dunmore*, (Virginia Independence Bicentennial Commission; Williamsburg, Va. 1977), p. 19.

102 Wainwright, ed., "Turmoil at Pittsburgh: Diary of Augustine Prevost, 1774," 143.

103 This incident, as well as the events leading up to it, are described by Mollie Gillen in *Royal Duke: Augustus Frederick, Duke of Sussex (1773–1843)*, (London, 1976), 135–136.

104 F. Scott Fitzgerald, *The Last Tycoon* (Scribner eBook edition, New York, 2003), Kindle loc. 3200.

105 See "Deposition of Patrick Henry in the lawsuit of Margaret Eustace vs. Seth John Cuthbert," *Blair Family Papers*.

106 Ebenezer Hazard, "MS Journal of Journeys to the South," in *We Were There*, p. 38.

107 In a February 26, 1777 letter to George Washington, Charles Lee wrote, "Eustace I consider as my adopted son, considering the circumstances of his being taken out of other [i.e., Lord Dunmore's] hands and his affection for me, I ought to look upon him in this light – in short, should any acci-

dent happen to me, it has long been my resolution to leave everything I possess on this side of the water, between these two young men [Eustace and Jacob Morris]" Charles Lee to George Washington, 26 Feb. 1777, *George Washington Papers at the Library of Congress, 1741–1799*: Series 4. General Correspondence. 1697 to 1799., http://memory.loc.gov (accessed 1 Jan. 2010) (See also, Major John S. Eustace to Charles Lee, 24 Aug. 1779, "The Lee Papers, 1778–1782, [vol.] III" pp. 362–364, 364.

[108] Kitty Eustace Cuthbert to Charles Lee, 10 Aug. 1779,. "The Lee Papers, 1778–1782, [vol.] III" published in *Collections of the New York Historical Society for the Year 1873*, (New York, Printed for the Society, 1874), pp. 355–356

[109] The fact that Kitty's P.S. survived and the letter to which it was attached did not, suggests that the P.S. was a treasured object and that her question, "How comes it you never Courted me?" might not have been taken (or intended) as merely rhetorical.

[110] John Skey Eustace to Charles Lee, 28 Nov. 1779, "The Lee Papers, 1778–1782, [vol.] III," p. 395.

[111] John Skey Eustace to Charles Lee, 12 Dec. 1779, "The Lee Papers, 1778–1782, [vol.] III," pp.396–398. In the same letter, Eustace told Lee that if he had his "passions under a[s] perfect control as they had [him] there would not be his equal on earth" for strict goodness, greatness and honesty, *ibid.*, p. 398.

[112] In the 1800 Federal Census for Wallkill, New York, Margaret Eustace is described as the head of a family of three males, two slaves and one white. If Kitty gave birth to a boy in 1779, he would have been just old enough to be listed in the Census as a "white male from 16 to 26," the category in which the while male living in the Eustace household is classified. (It is also possible that the nameless white male was the son of John Skey Eustace by an equally nameless woman.)

[113] That Seth John Cuthbert was as well-connected as he was argues strongly against him embracing the status of a bigamist. As we know Mary Clay Cuthbert had her first child by him in 1785, and as it is not unlikely that Kitty's bereaved husband took a year or two to pop the question, the *terminus ad quem* for Kitty's death could be as early as 1780.

[114] Catherine Blair to Thomas Burke, 18 Nov. 1774, *Thomas Burke Papers.*

[115] As with so many other, similar ejaculations by John Skey Eustace, the title says it all.

[116] "Eustace is a strange figure whose biography remains to be written."

Melanie Randolph Miller, *Envoy to the Terror: Gouverneur Morris and the French Revolution*,(Dulles, Va., 2005), p. 128.

[117] John Skey Eustace, "Treaty of Friendship of Commerce and Navigation between His Brittanic Majesty and the United States of America, Finally Ratified by the American Legislature, Followed By a Fraternal Project," (Paris, 8 July 1796), as translated from the French by Jon Kite, Ph.D. (I would here like to thank Dr. Kite for his invaluable assistance as a researcher, translator and guide to the vagaries of French military terms).

[118] Margaret Crawford Jackson, "The Town of Hamptonburgh" in *The History of Orange County New York*, ed. Russel Headley (Middleton, N. Y., 1908), p. 514

[119] *Norton Critical Edition of Tristram Shandy*, Howard Anderson, ed. (New York, 1980) p. 276.

[120] *Ibid.*, p 457.

[121] Besides Jefferson and Adams, Alexander Hamilton and Benjamin Franklin are both known to have owned copies of *Tristram Shandy*, as did a number of prominent Virginians, including Jefferson friends George Wythe and Robert Carter. It may be worth noting that this admittedly unrepresentative list includes a vegetarian (Wythe), a refugee from the Church of England (Carter), three Deists (Jefferson, Hamilton and Adams) and a member of the Hellfire Club (Franklin.) Exactly how *Tristram Shandy* contributed to the moral and intellectual development of these men remains to be determined.

[122] See John Adams to Abigail Adams, 16 Mar. 1777, *Founding Families: Digital Editions of the Papers of the Winthrops and the Adams*, C. James Taylor, (Boston: Massachusetts Historical Society, 2007). http://www.masshist.org/ff/ (accessed 10 Jan. 2010.) In 1788, Jefferson returned to *Tristram Shandy* for suitable words to revive his affair that was not an affair with Maria Cosway. (The passage he quoted was Sterne's obscene improvisation on the subject of "noses." Mrs. Cosway was not amused.) Thomas Jefferson to Maria Cosway, 24 Apr. 1788, *The Papers of Thomas Jefferson*, Julian P. Boyd et al, eds, (Princeton, 1950–), 13: 103–104. On yet another occasion, Jefferson described *Tristram Shandy* as "the best course of morality that ever was written." See Kevin B. Hayes, *The Road to Monticello: The Life and Mind of Thomas Jefferson* (Oxford, 2008), p. 254. Jefferson's personal *bête noir*, Alexander Hamilton, invoked the same passage in asking his friend John Laurens (who was trying to find him a wife) to "do justice to the length of my nose." Alexander Hamilton to John Laurens, April 1779,

Harold C. Syrett, ed., *The Papers of Alexander Hamilton*, (27 vols.; New York: Columbia University Press, 1961–87), 2:37–38.

[123] Dr. Samuel Johnson called *Tristram Shandy* "too odd to last." *Boswell's Life of Johnson*, ed. George B. Hill, 2: 449. He was wrong. It has lasted quite well, despite being called "the first modern novel" a description that, in one case at least, has served as a launching platform for an illiberal (and altogether a-historical) attack on the novel as a "defeatist tale of the blighted and battered, of impotence and disfigurement." Terry Eagleton, *The English Novel, An Introduction*, (Malden, Mass.; 2005), p.92.

[124] *Norton Critical Edition of Tristram Shandy*, p.112

[125] Jane Austen, *Pride and Prejudice*, James Kinsley ed., (Oxford World Classics Paperback ed., Oxford, 2004), p. 278.

[126] Charles Dickens, *A Tale of Two Cities*, (London, Chapman and Hall, 1859), p. 1.

[127] Lawrence Sterne to Dr. John Eustace, 9 Feb. 1768 *The Works of Lawrence Sterne*, 6: 250–251.

A Few Words on Virginia Slavery and the Revolution

This is a series about a battle with irony as fierce as the Revolutionary War itself. It is also a series about the overwrought narratives Virginians fashioned to avert those ironies. Some of the Virginians' narratives – those in their letters, for example – were ostensibly private. Others, like Patrick Henry's speeches, Arthur Lee's Monitor essays, George Mason's *Declaration of Rights* and Thomas Jefferson's *Summary View of the Rights of British America* and the American Declaration of Independence, bear all the marks of full-dress theatrical performances. Whether they were speaking to an audience of one or a hundred, Virginians never forgot they were addressing posterity.

Edmund Morgan has said that Revolutionary-era Americans "allowed Virginians to compose the documents that founded their republic, and they chose Virginians to chart its course."[1] That is true. But if Jefferson's Declaration of Independence put words to the visioning of America it also imported to that vision as subtext the defining fact of life in Virginia: black African slavery. Slavery is not listed among Jefferson's self-evident truths. This was after all political propaganda. But the fact is, that without slavery, Jefferson would not have had the time or the leisure to imagine America.

This is not to give slavery credit as the atrocity which "sensitized" Virginians to the blessings of liberty.[2] It is however to

---

[1] Edmund Morgan, *American Slavery, American Freedom* (New York, 1975), p. 387.

[2] See Robert Middlekauff, *The Glorious Cause* (Oxford, 1982), p. 606

remind ourselves that nothing in 18th Century Virginia is conceivable without slavery. Slavery supplied white Virginians with half their net worth, nearly all of their labor and their most stressed paradox: that they were themselves English slaves.

So fiercely did white Virginians covet their liberty, so proud and powerful were they in disposing of their human property, that there seems to be no parallel for it anywhere, except perhaps in the time of Republican Rome, that golden idyll so beloved by classically educated Virginia gentlemen. Of course, the slaves in this latter-day idyll do not have names. Literacy being power in Virginia, the mark of individual slaves on history is a frail "X." Their status as enduring metaphor is however unassailable.

One of America's best critics, Richard Poirier, has described the "extravagances of language" in American letters as "an exultation . . . of consciousness momentarily set free." "The most interesting American books," he wrote, "are an image of the creation of America itself, of the effort . . . to 'Build therefore your own world.'. . . They are bathed in the myths of American history; they carry the metaphoric burden of a great dream of freedom – of the expansion of national consciousness into the vast spaces of a continent and the absorption of those spaces into ourselves."[3] Poirier was talking about American prose fiction; in particular, 19th-Century American novels. Whether the writings of 18th-Century Virginians were bathed in the myths of history he did not say. But certainly it is hard to imagine a more compelling image of the creation of America itself than Thomas Jefferson's Declaration of Independence – or one more devoted to building its own world.

To emphatically declare the right to liberty a self-evident truth even as he was continuing to hold (in his own words) "the

---

3 Richard Poirier, *A World Elsewhere* (Oxford and New York, 1966), pp. 7, 3;

[slavery] wolf by the ears" not only defied belief; it made a mockery of it.[4]

Yet Virginians did more than embrace the paradoxes of Jefferson's great dream, they added to them. Having blamed the British government for bringing slavery in America, they did not hesitate to blame themselves – with equal vehemence – for having failed to rise above their own "dissipative indolence."[5]

By the time this book opens, the Virginians had been in a bad mood for years. Most grew one cash crop, tobacco, commerce in which was exclusively limited to Great Britain. Barred by law from issuing their own currency and obliged to pay excessive prices for the latest fashions, they were incensed to find darned holes in their "new" stockings just arrived from London. They liked to say "an English pronunciation is best," but found English condescension intolerable. They hated "dependency"; but given the chance would gladly accept appointment to a crown office. Virginia society was not like that of the other colonies. It was more proud; it was also more English. Virginians were not like other Americans. They were "prodigious in spirit" – even the Bostonians said that.

"Prodigious in spirit", "the most spirited and consistent of any" – one delegate to the First Continental Congress called the Bostonians "mere milksops" compared to the Virginians.[6] First impressions are made to be changed of course and what was once said of all the delegates from Virginia, even the most conservative, would eventually be reserved for just one: Patrick

4   Thomas Jefferson, *Notes on the State of Virignia* (Charlottesville, 1783)
5   *The Diary of Colonel Landon Carter*, Jack P. Greene, ed. (2 vols., Richmond, 1987), 1: 512.
6   Quoted in George Morgan, *The True Patrick Henry* (J.B. Lippincott and Co., 1907); reprint, American Foundation Publications, Bridgewater, Va. 2000) p.157. The delegate was Joseph Reed.

Henry, Jr. That is too bad, not because Henry was any less than legend tells, but because what made him prodigious was his unique ability to give voice to the true spirit of America. Nor is it difficult to trace the origins of this spirit to the mental and physical landscape of Virginia: the widely-dispersed, largely self-sufficient farms and plantations, each of them a virtual "little city"; the sense of near total autonomy that left the Virginia planter free to perfect his tyranny over his slaves at the very moment he was reacting with indignation to British encroachments on his own liberty.[7]

Slavery made white planters rich; but it was a wealth counted in lives which could not be spent. Slavery degraded the slave; but like all absolute power it also weakened and corrupted the master, belying his affectations of moral superiority and defeating his attempts at economic independence. Slavery was evil; and slavery supplied the Virginians with a handy metaphor for British tyranny. In short, Virginia bequeathed America a definition of liberty as deeply conflicted as Virginia itself; one which was linked, both figuratively and in fact, to a despotism far worse than any practiced by Parliament.

A subtitle for this series might be "the untold story of an unknown revolution." But any reader expecting to encounter the usual stuff of which revolutions are made – war, political and social chaos, or a French-Revolution-style reign of terror – is in for a surprise. There was no British massacre in Williamsburg, accordingly, there was no cause for vengeance; no garrisoning of British troops in Virginia houses, and thus no reason to complain of oppression; no closing of Virginia's ports, and thus no need to punish an entire population for the acts of a few. Instead of a

7 Letter of Phillip V. Fithian to John Peck, August 12, 1774, *Journal and Letters of Phillip Vickers Fithian*, ed. Hunter Dickinson Farish (Williamsburg, 1957), p. 161, 238fn1.

Battle of Lexington and Concord there was a *threatened* march on Williamsburg, not by a British occupation force, but a ragtag collection of militia commanded by Patrick Henry. The first conflict of the war in Virginia was no Bunker Hill, just a sad mowing-down of British grenadiers at Great Bridge, a miserable village defended by a wretched fort called "the Hogpen." Had not Cornwallis retired to Yorktown in 1781, Virginians might have been bystanders to their own revolution.

But if Virginia's battle against tyranny seems to lack for excitement, it is not because Virginians lacked for patriotic fury. It is because their battle, enacted as it was on the stage of a slave colony, seemed so preposterous. Instead of mob action on Boston Common we have Thomas Jefferson's lifelong effort to "carefully avoid . . . every possible act or manifestation on [the] . . . subject [of slavery.]"[8]

This a series about a revolution that was destined from the start to be imperfect; about a place and a people who have yet to find their rightful place in histories of the period. Not all of these people were rebels. Not all of their actions can be described as revolutionary. The Virginians liked to argue; they liked to write even more, and often kept copies of their letters. Some of their letters now seem artful, some merely oblique and some (like those of Patrick Henry) so effortlessly transparent as to require us to imagine an audience to make them intelligible. Their value lies less in what they say than in how they enact the stressed ironies of life in Virginia. Virginians really did see themselves as actors on a stage, but it was a classic, not a Georgian stage, and they were not only the principal actors but a chorus reflecting on the meaning of their actions. To treat the Virginians' well-chosen words merely as a quarry for facts would be silly. Virginians used words to aggrandize.

8   Thomas Jefferson to George Logan, 11 May 1805, Paul Leiscester Ford, ed., *The Writings of Thomas Jefferson*, 10 vols. (New York, 1892–1899), 9: 141.

So what do Virginians' words tell us about them and their revolution? Among other things they tell us that for lack of good cause to rebel, Virginians seized upon a deeply unpopular royal governor, Lord Dunmore, and found in him a plausible caricature of everything they despised; that the prodigious spirit of the Virginians was both a reaction to and a predisposition for tyranny; and that if Williamsburg is the most studied 18th-Century city in the world, Virginia itself remains mostly unread.

It is not too late to put that to rights. The close reading of the letters and diaries of historical figures is not an arcane science, any more than say, the close reading of a novel. Nor must it lead to new approaches to Virginia itself, though it may challenge some old ones. This is not a history of Revolutionary Virginia, though it might qualify as a prospectus for one, being in part a meditation on a theme of neglect as revealed in the works of those historians who like to think of 18th-Century Virginia as a place far, far away; that is, anything but a slave colony. For some people, the discovery of Founder DNA in the descendants of slaves will always be a revelation.

The popularity of books like Joseph Ellis's *American Sphinx* suggests Americans are willing to reinvest in Virginia's Founders, even the fallen ones, as long as the story is well told. I hope so, as the story of Virginia and the Virginia Founders is the back story of America itself, a narrative less about a race of heroes than a few large souls laboring to transform irony into myth. My focus on those ironies should not be misunderstood. It is in fact a manifestation of my esteem. Like Gov. Francis Fauquier, who once incautiously told their lordships at the Ministry that he had "come to love these Virginians," I have found what I abhor inextricably entwine with what I most admire.

GEORGE MORROW

List of Illustrations

A Cock and Bull for Kitty

Acknowledgements

Dr. Samuel Johnson once said, "It is wonderful how a man will sometimes turn over half a library to make just one book." After ten years of nearly constant work on this series, I find that I have not only turned over half a library, but a good part of my life. New friends have become old ones. Some very good friends who read the essays in this series in their very earliest versions are now gone. Meanwhile, the library – I am speaking of the ever-expanding library of the internet – has only gotten larger.

It is impossible to name everyone who helped make this series, but some I must mention. There would be no series without the love, encouragement and help of my wife, Joan Morrow. But for the welcoming attitude, expert assistance and criticism of two truly fine historians of the period, Rhys Isaac and James Horn, I would still be trying to distinguish the forest from the trees. The encouragement I received from my two chief non professional readers, Joan and Terry Thomas, turned a mere collection of dates, people and events into a study of the character of Williamsburg. Other people who read one or more of the essays and made helpful comments include my 90-year-old aunt Rosemary Bauder, Paul and Joan Wernick, Richard Schumann, Michael Fincham, Ken and Judith Simmons, Fred Fey, Cary Carson, Jon Kite and Al Louer. I also wish in particular to thank Jon Kite for obtaining the French army dossier of John Skey Eustace and for translating one of Jack Eustace's overwrought pamphlets from the French. Richard Schumann ,

James Horn and Roger Hudson kindly consented to do prefaces for one of the booklets in this series. Al Louer and Paul Freiling of Colonial Williamsburg arranged for me to see Williamsburg from the roof of the Governor's Palace, a view that put time itself in perspective .

Those who are subscribers to the British quarterly, *Slightly Foxed*, described on its website as "The Real Reader's Quarterly," will recognize some similarities between the booklets in this series and that magazine. The resemblance is no accident. When I saw *Slightly Foxed* for the first time, I immediately realized that it was the perfect model, in size, material and design for what I was looking for. With that in mind, I contacted Andrew Evans at 875 Design, the English book design firm responsible for its appearance, and asked him if would be willing to take on this project. He said, "yes," and it was not long before he and I had assembled a team of people who not only seemed to know what I wanted but were able to give me something I never expected to find: new ideas on the subject matter. I especially want to thank Gail Pirkis, the publisher of *Slightly Foxed*, for recommending Roger Hudson as editor for this series. Roger is not only a highly accomplished writer in his own right, he is truly a writer's editor.

Sadly, the genial spirit who presided over the series, read and commented on virtually every booklet and guided me through its development, died while the series was still in production. I am speaking of Rhys Isaac, the Pulitzer Prize-winning author of what is still the best book ever written on late colonial Virginia, *The Transformation of Virginia*. Rhys' presence at our dinner table will be deeply missed. But he will also be missed from the profession of history, where his exuberant writing style and elegaic approach to the past daily gave the lie to the sour souls who think history is about settling scores.

As I began these Acknowledgments with a quotation from

Samuel Johnson I would like to end with one *about* Johnson. It was spoken by someone who did not know him well, but knew of him very well, William Gerard Hamilton. For me, it is Rhys Isaac's epitaph: " He has made a chasm, which not only nothing can fill up, but which nothing has a tendency to fill up. – Johnson is dead. – Let us go to the next best; – There is no nobody; – no man can be said to put you in mind of Johnson."

About the Author

GEORGE MORROW brings a lifetime of experience to bear on the characters of the people featured in this series. He has been a university instructor, lawyer, general counsel for a *Fortune* 100 company, the CEO of two major health care organizations and a management consultant. He received his academic training in textual analysis and literary theory from Rutgers and Brown Universities. He lives in Williamsburg with his wife, Joan, and two in-your-face Siamese cats, Pete and Pris.

April 29, 1765 marked
the debut of a man whom
Thomas Jefferson called
"the greatest orator that ever lived."

"I am ready to show my loyalty to King George III
with the last drop of of my blood"

The Greatest Lawyer
That Ever Lived

Williamsburg in Character No. 2

Coming December 2010

WILLIAMSBURG IN CHARACTER

"Tribal, atavistic forces were abroad, both in England and in the Thirteen Colonies, and in them the Enlightenment met its match."

From the Preface by Roger Hudson

Francis Fauquier   Norborne Berkeley,
Lord Botetourt

The Day They Buried Great Britain

Williamsburg in Character No. 3

Coming December 2010

WILLIAMSBURG IN CHARACTER

A Cock and Bull for Kitty

The Greatest Lawyer That Ever Lived

As great moments in history go, Patrick Henry's May 30, 1765 speech against the Stamp Act and calling for "a Cromwell" to stand up against George III has to rank near the top. It marked the debut of a man whom Thomas Jefferson called "the greatest orator that ever lived." It also gave (again according to Jefferson) the "first impulse to the ball of [America's] Revolution," thereby transforming what had been a largely academic debate over natural rights into a call to arms. Here it is, described with all the bombast that Henry's first biographer, William Wirt, was known for:

> It was in the midst of this magnificent debate, while he was descanting on the tyranny of the obnoxious act, that he exclaimed in a voice of thunder, and with the look of a god – Caesar had his Brutus – Charles the first, his Cromwell – and George the third – ("Treason," cried the speaker – "treason, treason," echoed from every part of the house. – It was one of those trying moments which is decisive of character. – Henry faultered not for an instant; but rising to a loftier attitude, and fixing on the speaker an eye of the most determined fire, he finished his sentence with the firmest emphasis) *may profit by their example*. If *this* be treason, make the most of it."

It was a good story. But was it true? Not even Wirt was sure. In fact, he had no sooner written these immortal words than he "began to doubt whether the whole [story] might not be fiction."4 Having previously secured the assistance of Thomas Jefferson for his "little literary project" and "[w]ith a view to ascertain the truth" from someone who was actually there that day, Wirt decided to submit the tale of Patrick Henry and the Speaker to "Mr. Jefferson as it had been given to me." No matter that 40 years had passed, no matter that Jefferson still bore a grudge against Henry for a 1781 inquiry into Jefferson's inept and, some said, craven conduct as wartime governor of Virginia. Jefferson would decide. And decide he did: "I well remember the cry of treason [Jefferson replied], the pause of mr. Henry at the name of George the III, and the presence of mind with which he closed his sentence, and baffled the charge vociferated."6 That was enough for Wirt: "The incident," he declared in a footnote to his *Sketches of the Life and Character of Patrick Henry*, "becomes authentic history."

And so the matter stood until 1921, when *American History Review* published a hitherto unknown eyewitness account of the incident found in the files of the French spy service.8 The writer of the scholarly introduction to the account noted that the anonymous author seemed to "use English and French with nearly equal freedom, at any rate spell[ed] both about equally well," but since the manuscript was "in the same hand throughout, with the same peculiarities of execution," he concluded that the account "was not the first manuscript, but . . .the result of subsequent copying." More recently, Rhys Isaac has suggested that the first manuscript was in fact the original manuscript and that the "Frenchman" was actually "a disaffected Irish Catholic," writing in his native tongue — thereby explaining why the Speaker's charge of "Treason!" became "traison" in the so-called "copy."9 As an Irishman, and thus a victim of English tyranny himself, it was natural that the spy would take an interest in a regicidal speech by any of George III's subjects, particularly one with a Scotch Irish name :

May the 30th. Set out early from halfway house in the Chair and broke fast at York[town], arrived at Williamsburg at 12, where I saw three Negroes hanging at the gallows for having robbed Mr. Walthoe of 300 ps. I went immediately to the assembly which was sitting. . . . Shortly after I came in one of the members stood up and said he had read that in former times Tarquin and Julius [Caesar] had their Brutus, Charles [the First] had his Cromwell and he did not doubt that some good American would stand up for his country, but (says he) in a more moderate manner, and was going to continue, when the speaker of the house rose and Said, he, the last that stood up had spoke traison, and [he, the Speaker] was sorry to see that not one of the members of the house was loyal enough to stop him before he had gone so far. Upon which the same member stood up again (his name is hennery) and said, that if he had affronted the speaker, or the house, he was ready to ask pardon, and he would shew his loyalty to his majesty King G[eorge] the third, at the Expence of the last drop of his blood but what he had said must be attributed to the Interest of his Country's dying liberty which he had at heart, at the heat of passion might have lead him to have said something more than he intended, but, again, if he said anything wrong, he begged the speaker and the houses pardon. Some other members stood up and backed him, on which that affair was dropped.

If Patrick Henry baffled (repelled) the charge of treason it was out of hearing of the Frenchman, whose account of Henry calling for an assassin for George III at one moment and offering to die for him the next was so matter-of-fact, anti-heroic and unexpected as to be credible on those grounds alone. Clearly, if what the Frenchman reported was not a complete retraction, it was the closest thing to it. No wonder the affair was dropped. It would be hard to imagine a more abject apology or a less heroic ending.

Was Henry a hero or a coward? Had he roared out defiance to King George III only to swallow his pride and along with it, the title of first mover of the American Revolution?